Many Christian leaders these days are talking about a "kingdom mind-set." If you wonder what this really means, you will find the answer in *God Out of the Box*. Chuck Ripka lives his life with a kingdom mind-set, and his enthralling real-life stories will help you reach higher than ever to fulfill your greatest possibilities!

—C. Peter Wagner
President, Global Harvest Ministries
Wagner Leadership Institute

These are critical times that require critical thinking. We must be confronted in a way that causes us to develop a mind-set that breaks us out of our normal conformed mold and transforms our mind to perceive God's best for our future. Chuck Ripka has written a wonderful book to help you get your mind thinking differently. This book reveals how the Lord led him on a journey that moved him and his family into a realm of faith that continues to this day. There is a power in hearing the Lord's voice, giving as we are instructed, and influencing others in society that causes the blessings of God to overtake our lives. *God Out of the Box* is a great book that will help you perceive how vast His thoughts are toward you and how He can unlock your potential to change the world around you!

—Chuck D. Pierce
President, Glory of Zion International, Inc.
Vice President, Global Harvest Ministries

Chuck Ripka's *God Out of the Box* is a testimony of a man who has moved from theory to the daily practice of experiencing God at work. I've enjoyed being a part of his journey, and I know you will be incredibly encouraged as you read his firsthand God-encounters in the workplace. Every workplace believer should read this book!

—Os Hillman, President
Marketplace Leaders and
International Coalition of Workplace Ministries

God Out of the Box is about a real person who is showered with blessings as a result of his obedience to God's Word and direction. Chuck Ripka portrays his witness to Christ through his everyday, ordinary experiences and translates these godly episodes into helpful direction for the ordinary person. This book is a must-read for everyone, no matter where they are in their life's journey.

—Lieutenant Governor James Duke
Honolulu, Hawaii

Chuck Ripka has an ability to tell God stories in such a way that you want to go out and help people experience God as he does. He is real, powerful, and impacting in his sincere love for God. Every marketplace minister in the world needs to read what this God practitioner has written.

—Cindy Jacobs
Generals International

Chuck is the most authentic person I know, which is why I count him as one of my truest friends. Every word that comes from his mouth is pure, anointed, and accomplishes what it is sent to do. It is for this reason that he has been entrusted with the high calling of prophet to the nations. Because of Chuck's deep humility and uncompromising obedience, God works with Chuck, confirming His word by the signs that accompany it. This book is the evidence of that, but the stories you will read are merely the tip of the iceberg. Daily, the Word continues to "increase and spread" (Acts 12:24) through Chuck's life as he overcomes the evil one by the blood of the Lamb and the word of his testimony and forcefully advances the kingdom of God.

—Graham Power
Chairman, Power Group of Companies,
Transformation Africa, and Global Day of Prayer

After over twenty years of formal education, I have read and heard enough theory! *God Out of the Box* is not theory. It is a captivating montage of real-life stories of how an ordinary person is continually visited, empowered, and guided by an extraordinary God. Prepare yourself for a feast! You will be well satisfied.

—PAUL L. COX
ASLAN'S PLACE

Successful banker and businessman Chuck Ripka has received a revelation that has the potential to bring radical transformation and renewal to our communities and to their educational, political, and business arenas. This revelation has resulted in governments and international business leaders seeking him out in order to receive an impartation of this wisdom. He has penned many of these truths in his book, *God Out of the Box*. As you peruse its pages, your passion for life and work will begin to be rekindled as you discover anew God's purposes and design for your existence.

—JACK FROST
FOUNDER, SHILOH PLACE MINISTRIES
AUTHOR, *EXPERIENCING FATHER'S EMBRACE* AND
FROM SPIRITUAL SLAVERY TO SPIRITUAL SONSHIP

When I came home from my first trip to Argentina people asked me what I learned there. I responded, "God is much bigger than I thought. He doesn't fit in the box that I had Him in." In other words, my own thinking had limited what God could do in my life. When God revealed Himself to me on this larger scale, He could then do exceedingly abundantly more than I had previously thought. In his book, *God Out of the Box*, Chuck shows us that God has given him this same revelation. I pray that as you read this book, God will open the eyes of your understanding and you will begin to see God at work in every aspect of your life.

—RICK HEEREN
AUTHOR, *THANK GOD IT'S MONDAY!*

Knowing and reading Chuck's story reminds me of why the Book of Acts does not have a formal closing. The marketplace miracles of two thousand years ago are still happening today! Chuck's ordinary life of the supernatural should inspire all of us that we can do the extraordinary when we pray and obey. If you want to experience a surge of faith, then this book is surely for you!

—RON LEWIS
SENIOR PASTOR, MORNING STAR NEW YORK (MSNY)
NEW YORK, NY

It is with great pleasure I write this endorsement for Chuck Ripka. In my opinion, Chuck is an inspiring man that lives what he believes and clearly understands the favor of God. His wife and family are a credit to him as he reaches for the next challenge the Lord has in front of him. I am blessed to know that I have had a small part in the journey of this great leader, knowing that he will be faithful with what he puts his hand to.

—DOUG STANTON
DOUG STANTON MINISTRIES INTERNATIONAL

Chuck Ripka is a unique person, and consequently this is the story of one man's unique journey filled with wonderful faith adventures and exciting ministry opportunities. But it is more than just a story. It also highlights lessons to be learned from Chuck as he listened to the voice of the Lord and then walked in obedience. You will be challenged as you read this book to do what he did, to trust God and in return to earn His trust. I heartily recommend this extraordinary book.

—DR. ALAN LANGSTAFF
APOSTOLIC OVERSEER, OMEGA TEAM, EXCELSIOR, MN

All we can say is, "Wow!" We laughed and we cried reading *God Out of the Box*. We know that everyone who reads this exciting story will be entertained, enriched, and increased in a hunger to know God on a deeply personal level. The lessons learned here in these chapters about simple obedience to God should inspire every reader first to listen, and then to obey! We all need to think about how our saying yes to God affects all those around us, and also the legacy that we leave for our children and our children's children! Certainly, Chuck is leaving a legacy of blessing.

—Pastors Jim and Ramona Rickard
Founders of Resurrection Apostolic
International Network (RAIN), Midwest
Apostolic Prophetic Conference,
International Healing Conferences,
and International Association
of Healing Ministries

Have you put God in a box and limited what He desires to accomplish in your life? If so, learn from Chuck's mistakes, victories, and wisdom. *God Out of the Box* is filled with powerful principles for living a victorious Christian life. When applied, you too will experience the truth—God has no limits! Sit back, relax, and enjoy encouraging stories told by a masterful storyteller. Chuck skillfully weaves words of affirmation, instruction, confirmation, dedication, warning, purpose, plans, innocence, and obedience with the overwhelming love of God.

—Tommi Femrite
President, GateKeepers International
Member, International Coalition of Apostles
Member, Eagles Vision Apostolic Team

Chuck's inspiring book charts the journey of an obedient servant and how the Lord has brought him into greater responsibilities as he has faithfully fulfilled even the smallest task. The Lord has remarkably opened doors for Chuck in the marketplace, government, and church. Chuck's enthusiasm for the Christian life and ongoing Spirit-led activity is contagious. His obedience challenges us to stop limiting what God wants to do in our lives. This compelling narrative will truly motivate us to magnify our Lord and His mighty deeds as we journey together.

—Larry J. Alberts
Presiding Elder, Way of the Lord Church
Overseer, Fathers and Families Together

I believe that there is a real desire placed in the hearts of people to hear the voice of God. This book is more than one man's dynamic story of working faith. It is an excellent model of how to hear God's voice and live out practical obedience to Him in everyday life encounters. I highly recommend this book to everyone who longs to have and make an eternal difference in life.

—Pastor Mike Smith
Redeeming Love Church
Maplewood, MN

Chuck Ripka is a friend who inspires me. One of Webster's definitions for inspiration is "one who is *moved to action*." *God Out of the Box* contains the stories of an ordinary man who obeyed an extraordinary God that will inspire you to a lifestyle marked by obedience. Inspiration guaranteed!

—Pastor Paul Salfrank
Alliance Community Church
Elk River, MN

GOD OUT *of* THE BOX

CHUCK RIPKA
with JAMES LUND

Charisma
HOUSE
A STRANG COMPANY

Most Strang Communications/Charisma House/Siloam/FrontLine/Realms products are available at special quantity discounts for bulk purchase for sales promotions, premiums, fund-raising, and educational needs. For details, write Strang Communications/Charisma House/Siloam/FrontLine/Realms, 600 Rinehart Road, Lake Mary, Florida 32746, or telephone (407) 333-0600.

God Out of the Box by Chuck Ripka with James L. Lund
Published by Charisma House
A Strang Company
600 Rinehart Road
Lake Mary, Florida 32746
www.charismahouse.com

Unless otherwise noted, all Scripture quotations are from the Holy Bible, New International Version. Copyright © 1973, 1978, 1984, International Bible Society. Used by permission.

Scripture quotations marked NKJV are from the New King James Version of the Bible. Copyright © 1979, 1980, 1982 by Thomas Nelson, Inc., publishers. Used by permission.

Cover design by studiogearbox.com

Author's Note: Incidents and persons portrayed in this book are based on fact. However, some names and details of the stories have been changed to protect the privacy of the individuals involved.

Library of Congress Cataloging-in-Publication Data

Ripka, Chuck.
  God out of the box / Chuck Ripka.
    p. cm.
  ISBN-13: 978-1-59979-056-5 (hardback)
  1. Christian life. I. Title.
  BV4501.3.R57 2007
  248.4--dc22

                                    2006030245

First Edition

07 08 09 10 11 — 987654321
Printed in the United States of America

DEDICATION

To my Father in heaven for loving and adopting me, for allowing me to sit on Your lap and hear Your voice clearly, and for showing me the way.

To my wife, Kathi, for coming alongside me so we can go through each God story together. I couldn't do it without you. I love you.

ACKNOWLEDGMENTS

I wish to extend a special thanks to the following people:

| The Servant Leadership team in Elk River, for being friends and co-laborers, especially my pastor, Paul Salfrank, Pastor Bob Pullar, Pastor Greg Pagh, Ken Beaudry, and Mayor Stephanie Klinzing.

| Ed Silvoso, for being like a father, stretching me spiritually, and stretching my vision of taking transformation to the nations. Thank you, Ed, for helping me take God out of the box!

| Cindy Jacobs, for her gift of prophecy, words of wisdom, and consistent encouragement to write this book.

| Stephen Strang and the entire team at Charisma House, for stepping out in faith to take on this project.

| Jim Lund, for his help with writing, organizing my thoughts, and crafting this book in a way that makes each story come alive for the reader.

| My wife, Kathi, for her wisdom, encouragement, and editing expertise.

| Each of my children and their spouses, for putting up with all the stories I have told over the years.

| All of the intercessors who have prepared the paths I have traveled.

| And finally, all of the people who are included in this book. It's been a pleasure to join with you in the amazing stories God is writing every day.

Contents

CONTENTS

FOREWORD

Can you imagine God coming to visit you every day for a chat—and for this to happen in your workplace? Wouldn't that be amazing? Envisage now that He comes by when you are "in the middle of something," one of the many challenging and occasionally annoying tasks that conform your daily routine and one that you are having trouble with. Wouldn't it be great to be able to ask for His advice or help? Life would definitely be better under those circumstances, wouldn't it?

This is not a far-fetched prospect at all. In Eden God had daily talks with Adam and Eve in the cool of the afternoon. He came to visit them in the garden, which was their workplace. The fact that God came down from heaven when it would be most comfortable weather-wise (in the cool of the day) suggests that this was meant to be a pleasant time. There is no record of what was discussed during those visits, but we know that at least they talked about horticulture, diet, and the naming of animals. Those daily visits were for the benefit of Adam and Eve as well as for the job they had been assigned to do. I am sure God also got great enjoyment, similar to grandparents playing with their grandkids. It is not what our grandkids can do for us, but it's the fact that we do it *together*.

This is also the case in the other encounters God had with humans in the Bible. Whether it was Abraham, Joseph, Moses, Joshua, Gideon, Daniel, Isaiah, Jeremiah, Hezekiah, and many others in the Old Testament, or Peter, Paul, and the disciples in the New Testament, the reason for those meetings was because there was a problem on the earth, and divine instructions, power, and anointing needed to be dispensed in order to deal with it. No human being was ever asked by God to do something in heaven. In fact, in those encounters He never brought heaven up at all.

The same is true today. God is deeply interested in what we do at work, and as I demonstrate in my book *Anointed for Business*, Jesus did not come to save just souls but everything that was lost, and this includes labor and the marketplace. Thanks to what Jesus actually redeemed on the cross, God can once again come down in the cool of the afternoon to fellowship with us and to dispense power to solve workplace problems.

Chuck Ripka, in his book, *God Out of the Box*, illustrates and demonstrates this with eloquence and clarity. In story after story Chuck shows that it is possible *and enjoyable* to take the presence and power of God to the workplace, not just occasionally, but every day of the week. And when we do, we come to love Mondays as much as we love Sundays.

Read, rejoice, be edified, and go change the world for Jesus!

—ED SILVOSO
FOUNDER AND PRESIDENT, HARVEST EVANGELISM
AUTHOR, *ANOINTED FOR BUSINESS*

INTRODUCTION

I am a simple, ordinary guy. I come from a poor family in Minnesota. My formal education ended in high school. I have no theological background or training.

Fortunately I am blessed that God makes faith in Him simple. He speaks to me often—not audibly, but in a way that I still recognize as His voice. At first, I thought everyone heard from the Lord the way I did. It was a long time before I realized this wasn't true. Now I see that people are desperate to talk to God. They hunger for an intimate, one-on-one relationship with their Creator.

Maybe you are one of them.

I talk to God all the time, and He answers me. I can't say that I understand why I'm blessed this way. But when He speaks, I listen. For more than twenty-five years, the Lord has been teaching me how to grow closer to Him. I have learned that it starts by acting on a single word with eternal significance: obedience.

From the moment the first man and woman walked on this earth, all that the Lord has desired from His children is their obedience. It is the foundation of a commitment to Him and the doorway to all the good things He gives to us.

When we trust God enough to obey Him in the little things, we earn His trust. And I have discovered that when God trusts us with the little things, it soon leads to His trusting us with bigger things. He begins using us in amazing ways. At the same time, our relationship with Him gets stronger and goes deeper.

I'll never forget the day God spoke to me after I counseled with Carl Pohlad, owner of the Minnesota Twins and my boss at the time. I sensed the Lord telling me these words: Chuck, I trust you.

I was stunned. I felt so honored to hear those words. "No, Lord," I said. "I trust You."

If you really trust Me, take Me out of the box you have set Me in. You limit Me in what I want to do in your life.

God had set me up. He was reminding me of all my doubts about what He'd said He would do. I still felt honored but also humbled. "OK, Lord," I said. "No more boxes."

Obedience and trust in the Lord have changed my life. They have taken me from my days as a twenty-year-old with no clue about his future to a forty-eight-year-old, happily married man who is "Dad" to five great kids and "Papa Chucky" to six grand-children. From a job as a construction worker (and not a very good one) to a position as an international banker. From helping launch a local bank to the beginnings of an international financial empire. From an empty life of wandering and searching to a life full of meaning and direction.

More importantly, the Lord is using my obedience and trust to change the lives of the people around me—in my family, my neighborhood, my church, my business, our schools, our city, and our state government.

The nations are next. I can't wait.

When the Lord speaks to me, I discover one amazing truth after another. That's part of what this book is about. It offers many principles I have learned from God that can change your world.

But I'm not a teacher; I'm a storyteller. And there's a story behind every one of these principles. I call them "God stories." I love to talk about what the Lord does when we obey and trust Him. You'll find many of His stories in this book. Some of the stories are amazing. Some can only be described as miracles. I tell them to everyone I know, and often to people I don't know. I can't stop talking about God. The reason is that every day of my life is filled with "divine appointments"—God stories waiting to happen.

God stories are waiting for you, too. If you obey and trust Him, you will see them. They're right around the corner. You can choose to enter into them or pass right by. I choose to enter into them.

INTRODUCTION

I may be a simple, ordinary guy, but I have an extraordinary God. He's working every day in my life and yours. He's a God that can't be kept in a box. He has no limits.

Let me tell you about Him.

Chapter One

BECAUSE *of* YOUR OBEDIENCE

Principle #1: God desires your obedience.

One of my favorite memories began on a warm, cloudless spring day when I was five years old. I always enjoyed the one-mile walk home from kindergarten in Melrose, Minnesota, the small town where I grew up. After a day in the classroom, I loved being outside, to be able to run and jump and play.

Each day I passed a park about two blocks from where we lived. On this particular afternoon, the dandelions were blooming. I couldn't help noticing the waves of yellow amidst the ocean of green grass. *Look at all the pretty little flowers,* I thought. Then inspiration struck. *I know! I'll pick some for Mom.* Soon enough, I gripped an enormous bouquet.

I loved to please my parents and hear their words of praise. It made me feel valuable and that I was contributing something to the family. I hurried home from the park. I couldn't wait to see my mother's face.

Mom was in the kitchen when I got home. With my surprise hidden behind my back, I walked right up to her. Suddenly I displayed the dandelions, nearly pushing them into her face, and announced, "These are for you!"

My mother was not a large person—she only stood four feet eleven inches tall and barely weighed one hundred pounds—but the smile that formed when she saw my flowers was big enough to light up the whole town of Melrose. "Chuckie, how beautiful!" she said, giving me a warm hug. "Thank you so much for thinking to bring me flowers." Immediately, she filled a large glass with water, placed the dandelions inside, and arranged them in the middle of the kitchen table.

I felt so proud for doing something to make my mom happy.

Unfortunately, most of my childhood memories were not as happy. Maddie Ripka, my mom, was a pretty, vivacious woman that everyone loved. Joe Ripka, my dad, was a hard worker who labored in the Kraft Foods factory in Melrose for more than forty years. But both of my parents were alcoholics, and their personalities changed when they drank. My mom transformed from spunky into belligerent. My dad frequently grew angry. The result was endless arguments and nasty fights.

I recall a summer night about two years after the dandelion surprise. My parents were out. My two brothers and I—Dan, two years older, and Russell, two years younger—had just crawled under the covers in our upstairs bedroom when we heard the door bang open downstairs.

"You drank too much again," my father said in a loud voice.

"*I* drank too much? Look who's talking," my mother snapped back.

We lived in what once had been a magnificent home built in the late 1800s, though it had fallen into disrepair by our time there. Each of the upstairs rooms had a round metal grate in the floor that allowed heat to rise from the bottom floor in winter. On this night, as I had on many other nights, I scrambled out of bed, pried off the grate, and stuck my head into the hole in the floor. Lying in this awkward position, I could easily hear every sound below. I could even see part of the kitchen.

What I heard wasn't pleasant. My father unleashed a string of obscenities, followed by, "What were you saying to that guy at the bar, anyway? I saw you talking to him."

My mother cursed back. "None of your business. It's a free country, Joe."

I felt a nudge to my ribs and turned my head. Dan, on my right, and Russell, on my left, were also prone on the floor, listening.

"None of my business? I'll tell you what my business is. If you don't—"

"Shut up, Joe. Just shut up."

"If you just didn't drink so much. That's why we have these problems. You always—"

"I said shut up! Quit telling me—"

"No, you shut up! If you don't shut up, I'm gonna teach you a lesson."

My heart beat double-time against my chest and the wood floor. Too many times before, after a terrible argument, I had seen the evidence of my father's anger—bruises on my mother's arms, or black eyes. I had watched her go out wearing sunglasses even when it wasn't sunny and heard her tell people she had fallen down the stairs.

Now my mother's voice changed. She wasn't talking tough anymore. She sounded frightened. "No, no, no, don't hit me! Don't hit me!" she cried.

I jumped up and ran downstairs, my brothers right behind me.

In the living room, my father stood close to my cowering mother, his right fist raised.

"Papa, stop it. Stop it!" Dan yelled. With my father distracted, I grabbed my mom's hand and pulled her toward the stairs.

"It's all her fault," my dad said, abruptly lowering his fist and his voice. "If she just wouldn't drink so much."

"I don't drink half as much as you, Joe Ripka!" my mom barked. The anger flashed back into my father's eyes. He stepped toward us.

"Mom, stop; you're just making it worse," I said, tugging at her hand and leading her up the stairs as quickly as I could. That was the end of the fireworks that night. Mom slept with us. By morning, all was forgotten—at least by my parents.

Our home life was chaotic; people today would call it dysfunctional. But my brothers, two sisters, and I didn't know any better. We figured this was how life was for most people. We were poor— my dad didn't earn much at Kraft—but we didn't think much about that either. I sometimes played baseball and ran track in my bare feet because I didn't have shoes. If we couldn't afford fuel oil to run the stove in the kitchen in winter, we piled on the blankets. We also used blankets to cover the shabby furniture and to hide the holes in the walls where the plaster fell off. One item we always seemed to have plenty of was blankets.

My parents were too preoccupied by their own troubles to spend time worrying about us kids. We had free rein. It was easy to sneak out of the house at night—no one bothered to check if we were still there. The only rule in our home was, "Just don't get caught."

With so little supervision, it probably is not surprising that my brothers and I got into our share of trouble and started drinking ourselves. I got drunk for the first time when I was in the sixth grade. It wasn't much later that I started hosting my own beer parties, either at our house or someplace else. I found I had a talent for putting on events and getting people together, and soon my friends were encouraging me to organize their parties, too. I even kept a keg in my room so I would always have beer on tap.

The drinking led to drugs and more trouble. We got to know the staff of the Melrose police department quite well. I still remember Mom answering the door and seeing a policeman there. She didn't ask, "What do you want?" She would ask, "Which brother do you want?"

Despite the lack of supervision, I still wanted to please my parents, just as I had that day with the dandelions. I somehow sensed that obedience mattered, that it was important to show respect for their authority over me. I often did the laundry and tried to clean up the house. By asking questions and experimenting, I learned how to bake when I was twelve; soon I was cooking meals for the family or friends that came over. I would call my mother at the local bar and say, "Mom, you can come home. I've got supper ready now."

I didn't feel neglected or that I had a harder life than anyone else. Mostly I just wanted to see my parents get along, and I wanted to have a good time myself. My motto was, "I'll try anything at least once."

Occasionally in my junior and senior high school years, though, I found myself feeling depressed. That was when I would take a long walk and talk to God. It wasn't that I had any kind of personal relationship with God or that I knew much of anything about Him. Most of my family never went to church or read a Bible. I went to a Catholic school through sixth grade, but that didn't make much of an impression on me.

Even though I had the sense that God was out there, I didn't know who He was or what He was about. But when I was down, there was no one else to talk to. So I would take a walk and ask, "God, why do my parents have to drink and fight all the time?" Or, "Why am I so lonely?"

Then, before I knew it, things would turn around. I would forget all about God and go back to partying.

It was at a party that I met Kathi. I was seventeen, and when I spotted the pretty brunette in the corner of the room I thought, There's a girl I want to meet. I sat down next to her; we ended up talking for the rest of the night. From then on we were almost inseparable.

We were married in the Catholic church in Osseo, Kathi's hometown, on February 17, 1979. At the reception, my parents got drunk and partied with my friends and us.

When I got married, I had just turned twenty years old. Kathi was already four months pregnant. We had no possessions, no money—we spent the $800 cash we received at the wedding on our first car, a 1967 Chevy Nova—and minimal career prospects. I was enrolled in a chef school, but when Kathi learned she was pregnant, I quit to take a bridge construction job.

My carefree life was changing in a hurry.

About a year later, still with no real idea of what I was going to do with my life, I got involved in a direct-sales business. I began reading positive-thinking books that talked about the power of God and how important it was to put Him first. It was the first time I ever considered the idea of God playing a role in my life.

That summer, I decided to attend a weekend sales convention in Arizona with my brother-in-law, Richard. I remember drinking pony beers in the car on the drive down. On Sunday, during the final session of the convention, the speaker presented the gospel message and invited everyone in the audience who had not already done so to stand and invite Jesus Christ into their lives.

OK, God, I thought. *I don't have a plan for my life, but I guess You do. If this is what it takes and what You want from me, then I'll do it—I'll give You my life.* Right there in the auditorium filled with hundreds of salespeople, I rose from my metal chair and committed myself to the Lord. As the speaker prayed, I glanced over and noticed that Richard was standing, too.

Neither of us had even a desire to drink beer on the way home.

Kathi could not believe it when I told her what we had done. As a child, she prayed to Jesus. But while growing up in a Charismatic Catholic family, her relationship with Christ became distant. Still, she came along when I joined a local Bible study group, and it wasn't long before she invited Jesus into her heart again. I didn't tell my parents about our spiritual transformation. I knew they wouldn't understand.

Actually, I didn't understand what was happening myself. Yet it felt right within me. I began studying the Bible for the first time. I read that believers were to "go and make disciples of all nations...teaching them to obey everything I have commanded you" (Matt. 28:19–20). And I read Jesus' statement, "If you love me, you will obey what I command" (John 14:15).

I thought a lot about those verses. I decided I wanted to be a part of God's plan. I wanted to submit to His authority and ask Him to guide me in my life. I remember the night I sat in bed reading the Bible, staring at the wood paneling on the wall, and contemplating what faith was all about. I decided to address God: "OK, Lord, if this is true—if You really mean this—then, Lord, use me. Speak to me."

It was a wonderful, peaceful moment. I had already invited Jesus into my heart. Now I was ready to trust Him fully, to give Him complete control over my life. I had no theological training and had rarely set foot in a church. My understanding of the Word of God was still minimal. But I did have a childlike faith. It was all I needed.

A few weeks later, after just finishing a project at home, I sat down on the couch in the living room. It was a hot summer day. Suddenly I sensed the Lord speaking to me. It wasn't an audible voice, but inside my head it was just as clear as if someone was standing next to me and talking.

Chuck, the voice said, *you are going to have four or five children. And if you'll have them, I promise I will provide for all of them.*

I didn't have to think about it or wonder where the voice was coming from. I knew in my heart that it was God. *Wow,* I thought. *That's pretty amazing. Thank You, Lord, for speaking to me and giving me that promise.* I told Kathi, and we agreed with His plan for our lives. I also described my message from God to several of my family and friends. I could tell some thought I might be a little crazy. Some of them pointed out that we couldn't afford that many kids, but we believed in and trusted God. I knew what I heard.

God began speaking to me at other times too, giving me specific instruction or direction. It was exciting to feel I was growing closer to God. But life still offered many challenges. One of them was watching the steady deterioration of my mother.

Mom had been in and out of alcohol treatment centers for years. They never seemed to accomplish anything—patients regularly found ways to sneak in booze. Now all the years of drinking and smoking were catching up to her. Maddie Ripka was forty-five years old by the time I was twenty-three, but she looked and must have felt more like seventy-five. Seeing this tough and bubbly Scottish-Irish firebrand waste away was heartbreaking, but we didn't know what to do about it.

Mom, as mother of the bride, was to be one of the honored guests at my sister Deb's wedding that July. But on the morning of the ceremony, she was stretched out on her couch, drunk and suffering severe stomach pain. She couldn't go.

When my brother Dan checked on my mother later that day, he found her in a coma. An ambulance rushed her to the local hospital, then to the larger facility in St. Cloud. She weighed just seventy-five pounds.

When Kathi and I visited, Mom was still in the coma. Her doctor said her liver and kidneys were shutting down. The alcohol was finally overwhelming her system. She didn't have long to live.

It was a sad time for the entire family. It seemed a terrible end for a woman who had already lived through so much hardship and pain.

Two days later, I was driving home with Kathi after attending a Fourth of July celebration. We were talking about Mom; I felt especially downhearted. Suddenly, right there on Interstate 94, I sensed the Lord speaking to me again: *Chuck, I want you to pray with your mom before she passes away. It's not too late. Pray with her to invite Christ into her life.*

That wasn't a message I wanted to hear. Even though I knew time was short, I was extremely uncomfortable with the idea of trying to pray with my mother. Except for Kathi, I had never prayed with anyone before, and certainly not about anyone's salvation. I knew it would be awkward, that I wouldn't know what to say. And she was in a coma, anyway. I doubted she would even hear my words.

But I also remembered the words of Christ: "If you love me, you will obey me." I had given my life to Him. I realized just how important obedience was to God.

Still, I felt I needed some kind of sign. *Lord, she's in a coma*, I prayed. *If this is You speaking to me, I'll go to the hospital tonight. But to know this is You, I need her to come out of her coma. I need to see her say yes.*

I explained to Kathi that we had to make a stop. It was almost 11:30 p.m. by the time we got to Mom's room at the hospital. I stood next to her bed and took her hand. Her skin was a pale gray, her dark hair matted down on her head. An IV machine pumped fluids into her body through a vein in her arm. A clear, plastic oxygen mask covered most of her face. Even with the oxygen, her breathing was shallow.

I leaned closer. "Mom, wake up," I said.

I shouldn't have been surprised; she opened her eyes.

I didn't waste any time. "Mom," I said, "the Lord just spoke to me. He told me you've lived a hard life. But it's not too late. Would you be willing to ask Jesus Christ for forgiveness of your sins and invite Him into your life?"

Mom squeezed my hand.

I was nervous, but I closed my eyes and began to pray: "Lord, we know that You are right here in this hospital room with us tonight, and we thank You for always being ready and willing to welcome us into Your family." I looked at my mother. "Mom, do you confess all of your sins to Jesus Christ and ask Him to forgive you?"

She moved her head up and down slowly: yes.

I swallowed. "Mom, do you now ask Jesus Christ to come into your heart as your Lord and Savior?"

Again, she nodded yes.

Amidst the cloud of helplessness and despair that filled the room, hope suddenly crackled into the air like a lightning bolt. But I had to be sure.

"Mom," I said, leaning even closer and peering intently into her hazel eyes, "do you understand what I've been saying?"

For a moment, I thought I saw her eyes glisten. Once again, she nodded her head. I looked at Kathi standing next to me. Her eyes were moist, too. But she was smiling.

A few minutes later, Mom slipped back into the coma. But I was more than satisfied. God had given Mom—and me—the best gift I could imagine. As we walked out, I thanked the Lord for His mercy.

He answered, *Chuck, because of your obedience, I promise you I will give you all of your family.*

I knew what He meant. No one in my immediate family had a personal and intimate relationship with the Lord. But God was telling me that each of them would learn to put their trust in Him. Now I was even more overjoyed—and grateful that I had listened and obeyed.

My mother never did regain consciousness. The next week, just after Kathi and I happened to stop at the hospital for another visit, Mom left all her troubles and her earthly body behind. I cried, but I also rejoiced, because I knew where she had gone. And I looked forward to the day when we could begin making new memories together in eternity.

Since my mother died, the Lord has spoken more to me about obedience. He has pointed out that from the beginning of time, since the days of Adam and Eve, all He has asked from His children is their obedience. God has told me that He can take all of Scripture and make it so simple and clear that it can be described in one word. I thought that word would be *love*. I was wrong. The word is *obedience*. It is the foundation of a commitment to the Lord and the doorway to all the good things He gives to us. Now I believe I understand the meaning behind the message of Christ: "If you love me, you will obey me."

Chapter Two

GETTING COMFORTABLE

*Principle #2: Get comfortable with
being uncomfortable for God.*

It was a hot Tuesday in late July, and our first child was already ten days overdue. Kathi was definitely uncomfortable and more than ready to deliver. As her contractions increased overnight, we knew that our baby could arrive at any moment.

The next morning we checked into the downtown Minneapolis medical center. Meanwhile, I was a nervous father-to-be. After all, I was only twenty. *Will I be a good dad?* I wondered. *Am I ready for this kind of responsibility? Will the delivery go OK? What kind of life is my son or daughter about to begin?*

We settled into the delivery room. As the hours passed, I tried to encourage Kathi. Unfortunately, I didn't seem to be doing a very good job. I rubbed her back: "No, Chuck," she said, "that's too hard." A few minutes later, I rubbed a different spot: "No, that's not hard enough." I brought Kathi a cup of water with ice, but she just shook her head at me: "No, Chuck. No ice."

In between trying to help Kathi and talking with doctors and nurses, I kept watch on the clock. Our situation was complicated by the fact that I had just begun a job in bridge construction. It included health insurance—which we desperately needed—but the only way our new baby could qualify for coverage was for me to complete a carpenter apprentice class by the required date. The class was being offered just two more times before the deadline— that night and the following evening.

If our baby was born quickly, I knew I had the option of attending the first class that night. As afternoon dissolved into early evening, however, it became clear that Baby Ripka wasn't going to cooperate.

Oh, well, I thought. *I'll just go tomorrow night.*

What we didn't know then was that Kathi was trying to deliver a breech baby. The baby was trying to come out feet first. We were in for a long wait.

Wednesday night turned into Thursday morning. Then early afternoon. Then late afternoon. Kathi was wiped out. She had been in labor for more than thirty hours.

Finally, the clock showed 5:45 p.m. Our baby had made progress, but it appeared Kathi still wasn't ready to deliver. "Honey," I said as gently as I could, "I have to go to that class."

Even in her exhausted state, my wife was gracious. She understood how badly we needed the health insurance.

In the doorway, I turned to look at her one more time.

"Hurry," she said.

For the next two hours, my body may have been in a classroom, but my mind and spirit were in a birthing room a few miles away. What I didn't know was that while I was gone, the doctors concluded that a normal delivery wasn't going to happen. They decided to perform a Caesarean section.

Everything turned out well. Tanner, as we chose to name our son, was a healthy six-pound, five-ounce baby boy, and Kathi recovered fully from the surgery. But I was disappointed about one thing: I wasn't there when he was born. I missed the birth of my first child by only twenty minutes.

Then there was my job situation. I had no formal career training. Kathi's uncle had called in a favor to get me the bridge construction job, but I knew it wasn't a long-term solution. I wasn't as fast as the other, more experienced workers, and I didn't enjoy drinking and smoking with the rest of the guys when our shift ended. I just didn't fit in.

I stayed with it for the next year, and this time was able to be in the room when our second child, Rachel, was born. But soon after, with winter approaching and the construction business dwindling, I was laid off.

Our finances, of course, tightened up in a hurry. I found part-time work potting plants at a local nursery, selling coffee and vacuums, and helping out at furniture auctions. But it wasn't always enough to pay the bills. I remember going to the grocery store one day with ten dollars in my pocket. It was all we had. I needed to divide it so I could buy milk and bread, but also have enough to buy gas so I could make it home.

I had a wife, two kids, no real job, and almost no experience. This wasn't exactly what I had in mind when I gave my life to Jesus. It was a period of testing for my new faith.

"Hey, God," I prayed. "If You are real, then this is definitely a time when I could use Your help."

I somehow sensed that He wanted me to trust Him and be patient. But I wasn't too comfortable with the circumstances He had left me in.

Kathi experienced another kind of discomfort a few months later. We were at home in the evening when she suddenly put her hand to her head and sat down.

"What's the matter?" I asked.

"I feel faint," she said.

We didn't know it then, but Kathi had in fact undergone an incredibly rare ovarian pregnancy, followed by a miscarriage. And now she was suffering from internal bleeding.

Days passed. Kathi went through more pain and scheduled a doctor's appointment. On the morning of the appointment, however, she seemed better. "I feel pretty good," she told me. "I think I'll cancel that appointment." She knew we didn't have insurance and couldn't really afford the visit.

"No," I said, not wanting to take a chance. "You better get down there and get checked out."

Kathi called about two hours after she left for the appointment. I could hear the tension in her voice.

"Chuck, you need to hurry and get down here," she said. "I'm going into emergency surgery."

"Now what, Lord?" I prayed as I drove to the hospital. "This time we really need You."

The doctors found a quart of blood in Kathi's abdomen. They conducted test after test trying to determine what was wrong. Finally, they diagnosed the ovarian pregnancy. But it wasn't until Kathi's eighth day in the hospital that they realized we didn't have insurance.

A doctor, concerned about Kathi's high fever, ordered a cooling blanket. "Don't worry," he said. "I'm sure your insurance will cover it."

"Wait a minute," Kathi said. "We don't have any insurance." We informed the hospital staff of our situation when we checked in, but somehow that detail had not been passed on to the doctors. They were shocked.

Yet the Lord was watching out for us. Since Kathi's condition was so rare, the doctors asked her to sign a release form allowing them to document everything as a study case. In return, they agreed to waive most of their fees.

Even so, we faced a hospital bill of more than $67,000. But after we sat down with a county agent to work out an agreement and she learned I had no regular job and we had no savings, the state ruled that we didn't have to pay a penny.

God's timing, as usual, was perfect. Two weeks later, I was hired to drive a truck for a spring water company. That went so well that I was invited to join their sales staff. I worked hard, and before I knew it, I was making more money each week than my manager.

Apparently he didn't care for the change in our financial positions. He reduced my commission. I worked harder and made almost as much as before. My manager cut my commission again. And then again.

When he decided to reduce my commission a fourth time, I was really upset. I had had enough. I felt it was time to go, and Kathi agreed. Once again I was in the uncomfortable position of being without a job and needing to support my six-member family. Once again I was stretching my faith, depending on God to point me toward a solution.

Soon after, He did just that. I sensed Him say to me, *Chuck, go look in the newspaper. There's a job there for you.*

I found a newspaper ad for a sales opening at a Levitz furniture store. I wondered, *Was this what the Lord meant?* I'd never even been in a furniture store, but I had some sales experience. I figured, *Why not?*

After three interviews, they hired me, again on commission, for a sixty-day probationary period. I was excited and thankful to God for giving me this new opportunity. During that first month I sold as much furniture as the store's top sales staff. "Chuck, forget the probation," my manager said one day. "You're hired."

Another salesman there, a man named Dupree, was a strong Christian. We began having breakfast together about once a week at a small café in St. Paul.

"You know, Chuck," he said one morning over scrambled eggs, "you're an evangelist. That's your calling."

I had heard that term before, but I was still new to Christianity. I didn't really know what it meant. "Just what is an evangelist?" I asked.

Dupree explained that an evangelist is simply someone who talks to others about the gospel and shows them the way to faith in Christ. Though I had never led anyone to Jesus other than my mother, something about Dupree's words resonated inside me. *Yeah*, I thought. *That makes sense. That is me.*

One morning, just as I was walking in the door at work, the Lord confirmed Dupree's words. *Chuck*, He said, *someday you're going to pray with a customer.*

OK, Lord, I answered. If I had thought much about it, I probably would have been nervous. I had never prayed with a stranger before. But "someday" was a long way off. I didn't worry about it. I just concentrated on selling furniture.

Then, about three months later, I spotted a man walking into the store. He looked about forty. He wore jeans and had brown hair falling over his ears. I stepped in his direction.

Suddenly the Lord spoke to me: *Chuck, this is the customer you're going to pray with.*

Immediately I felt anxious. Though I was working again, our family was still struggling to make ends meet. My sales at the store had declined recently, and since my salary was based entirely on commission, if I didn't sell furniture, I didn't get paid.

"Lord," I prayed, "I can't. I'm on commission, and I'm having a bad week. I can't afford for him to walk out."

It wasn't just fear of losing a sale, though. The idea of praying with someone I'd never met scared me. *Lord, I don't know how to do this. What if he laughs at me? What if he gets mad?* I tried to think of more reasons for avoiding the whole idea. I didn't want to look foolish. I was nervous. I was uncomfortable.

I heard no answer to my long list of excuses. That made me uncomfortable, too.

The man was walking in my direction, his eyes roving to a section of mattresses.

OK, Lord, I thought with a sigh. *I'll do this. But I need Your help. If You open the door, I'll open my mouth.*

"Good afternoon," I said to the man. "Can I help you?"

He smiled, but when he spoke he seemed distracted.

"Um, yes," he said. "I'm here to buy a mattress."

"Well, we have a great selection here," I said. "I'm sure we can find what you're looking for."

I led the man down an aisle, and soon we were discussing mattress features and prices. After a few minutes, the man—his name was Craig—sighed.

"My wife has our old mattress," he said. "Actually, she's my ex-wife. We just divorced. Now I have custody of the kids." He proceeded to describe the breakup of his family and the struggles of being a single parent to three children. He felt as if his life was falling apart.

Suddenly he flashed a weary grin. "Sorry. I don't know why I'm telling you all this. I came here to buy a mattress."

I was still nervous, but I knew what I had to do. I sat down on the mattress we had been looking at. *All right, Lord,* I thought. *The door is open. Here goes.*

"Craig," I said, "I think I know why you're really here. The Lord spoke to me three months ago and said someone like you was going to come into the store. He said I was supposed to pray with that customer and help him invite Jesus Christ into his life. When you walked into the store today, the Lord told me that you were the one."

"Well, I'm already a Christian," Craig said. "You know, I believe I'm a good person."

Lord, I prayed in my heart, *give me the right words. Open his heart to receive Your Word.*

"Craig, being a good person does not qualify you for eternal life. But becoming a Christian takes only a simple step. You just need to ask Jesus to forgive you for all your sins, believe in Him, and invite Him into your life. Would you like to do that?"

Craig studied me for a moment. He didn't laugh or head for the nearest exit. He seemed to be weighing what I said.

"All right," he finally said in a quiet voice.

We bowed our heads. I prayed for Craig to seek forgiveness for his sins and to ask Jesus to come into his life. He agreed with every word.

"Thank you, Chuck," he said when we were done. He shook my hand. "Thank you so much."

Then Craig did another important thing—he bought a mattress from me. I was excited. I overcame my reluctance, obeyed the Lord, led a man to Christ, and finally made a sale. And again, God spoke to me: *Chuck, I have proven to you that you are going to be able to do ministry and business at the same time.*

I knew what He meant. I was uncomfortable with the idea of praying for strangers and mixing the Lord's work with my work. God was telling me I didn't have to be uncomfortable and that my work and His work were really all part of the same plan. If I was obedient, He would give me the words and take care of my needs. I had nothing to worry about.

I guided Craig to our checkout counter, where we said our good-byes. Then I took a little walk. I thought about the peaceful look on Craig's face after I prayed with him. And I thought about the sale I just made. A wonderful feeling of peace swept over me. The anxiety I felt less than just a few minutes earlier had melted away.

I smiled as I prepared to meet another customer. I was more comfortable already.

Walking with God does not translate into a life on easy street. Outwardly, we may experience just as many troubles as before, maybe even more. Yet we are changed on the inside. Our hardships can actually be beneficial. As Scripture says, "Consider it pure joy, my brothers, whenever you face trials of many kinds, because you know that the testing of your faith develops perseverance" (James 1:2–3).

The Lord doesn't say He will take away all our problems, but He does promise to walk with us every step of the way and guide us to the right path. And that leads to "the peace of God, which transcends all understanding" (Phil. 4:7).

After more than twenty years, I'm still learning how to get comfortable with being uncomfortable for His sake. But it's slowly growing easier. If you trust Him, I believe it will get easier for you, too.

Chapter Three

"Stop Praying for Roger"

Principle #3: Stop praying only for
others. Start praying with them.

As a young family, we had a small house on the outskirts of town. Our five kids romped around the house or outside in the yard. Tanner, our oldest, often played with a boy in our neighborhood named Robbie. It was in many ways a peaceful setting for our family and neighbors. But trouble was on its way.

It arrived suddenly one afternoon when Robbie's mother, Carrie, came home and found her husband, Roger, passed out in the bathroom from a stroke. An ambulance whisked Roger to the hospital, where he regained consciousness. But he faced an intense period of rehabilitation to repair the damage. When I returned home from work the next day, Kathi told me what happened.

I actually never met Roger, but I was certainly concerned for him. It was another reminder of how short life can be. I promised myself that I would pray for him the next morning.

I kept my promise. After breakfast, I was downstairs on my knees in our partially finished basement. I made my usual round of prayer requests—for myself and for continued success at the furniture store where I worked, for Kathi and her health and protection, and for each of my kids.

Then I got to Roger. "Lord, please be with Roger," I said. "Bless him with Your comforting presence. Heal his body, and use this time to bring Roger closer to You."

Suddenly, I felt what was starting to become a familiar sensation: the Lord was speaking to me. And His words made no sense at all.

Stop praying for Roger.

I was confused. "Lord," I said, "aren't we supposed to pray for the sick?"

Yes. But I want you to stop praying for *him because I want you to pray* with *him.*

I knew that God wanted me to get more comfortable with being uncomfortable for Him, but praying with strangers was still extremely difficult for me. I didn't want to look foolish. I didn't want to be rejected or ridiculed. I desired to please God, but at that moment, it just felt like too much.

"Lord, I'm not comfortable with this," I said. "You want me to drive to the hospital to meet a man I don't know. I sense You want me to pray with him to invite Christ into his life."

The more I thought about it, the more unfair it seemed.

"Lord, I can't do it. I won't."

There was no response. The room was silent. I felt my heart pound as I waited for an answer.

The Lord's silence spoke louder to me than a thousand words.

"All right, Lord," I finally said. "I'll do this. But can Kathi come with me? She has at least met Roger."

No. You must go alone.

Obviously I wasn't going to win this argument.

I went upstairs to tell Kathi that the Lord had just instructed me to pray with Roger. The first thing she said was, "And I'm not supposed to come with you."

Kathi frequently has a strong sense of God's will. Her statement was a confirmation to me that this was more than my imagination. I really had heard from God.

People ask me, "How do you know that what you're hearing is God's voice?" One way is the signs He gives me. He might tell me to go to a certain verse in the Bible, and that scripture will line up exactly with the words I've just heard. Or He'll confirm His message through an insight from my wife or someone else that they couldn't possibly have known unless it was from Him.

I often ask the Lord for signs to confirm His words. I don't ask for miracles, but for specific actions or circumstances that show I am on the right track. Gideon did it twice with a fleece, first asking God to leave dew on the fleece, then asking Him to make it dry. (See Judges 6:36–40.) He wanted to know for certain that God was calling him to lead the people of Israel. Likewise, I lay out a lot of fleeces. I want to know for sure.

A reporter once said to me, "You can't ask for signs. You're testing God." But I am not testing God. I am testing myself. To get from one city to another, a person needs road signs to point him in the right direction. That is all I ask for. If I shouldn't ask, why does the Lord keep giving me the signs?

Of course, sometimes His signs lead to places I would rather not go. That was the case with Roger.

That evening, I reluctantly drove to the hospital and peeked into his hospital room. It was filled with family and friends. Roger himself was in bed, nodding at the words of an older woman who might have been an aunt. His face was pale.

Lord, what am I doing here? I thought. *I don't know any of these people. And I can't pray with Roger in the middle of such a crowd.*

I walked in anyway and introduced myself. After a few moments, the crowd went back to talking to each other. I stood there, feeling alone and fidgeting with the Bible I purchased for Roger. Then a nurse came in.

"Sorry, everyone, but it's time to go," she said. "Roger needs to take a shower and get to bed so can get the rest he needs."

As the group began to break up, I moved alongside Roger's wife.

"Carrie, I can't leave yet," I said. "I really feel that I'm supposed to talk to your husband."

She stared up at me for a moment. I could only guess what she was thinking. But she knew Kathi, so she must have decided I wasn't completely crazy.

"Let's go downstairs to the cafeteria while Roger takes his shower," she finally said. "Then you can come back and talk to him."

I ordered a Coke at the hospital cafeteria. We sat down, and I explained how God had told me to pray with Roger.

"He won't do that," Carrie said, shaking her head. "I'm the religious backbone of this family. I know my husband, and I know he won't pray with you."

I took a deep breath. I did not want to be here. Yet I sensed that the Lord wanted me to persist.

I leaned forward. "Carrie," I said, "I know he'll pray with me. Every time God has sent me to pray with someone, that person has said yes. I'm only asking that you let me try."

Carrie focused on the table for a moment. Then her eyes locked on mine. "All right. You can try."

Back in the hospital room, I pulled a chair over to Roger's bed. Carrie stood behind me. Roger's face had more color now, but I could see the worry in his frown.

I smiled and spoke quickly. "Roger, I'm Chuck Ripka, your neighbor. I know you are facing an extended period of rehabilitation, and I'd like to pray with you." I explained how I'd been praying for him that morning and that God had told me to come pray with him instead. It sounded strange as I said it. I paused, fearing that Roger would tell me to stop, or leave, or worse. The frown remained, but his expression didn't change.

"Roger, the Lord loves you. He wants you to be a part of His family right now," I said. "Would you be willing to pray with me and invite Jesus Christ into your life?"

Roger blinked. His eyes flitted to Carrie behind me, then back to me. He pulled himself up a couple of inches in the bed. "All right," he said.

I led Roger through the sinner's prayer, and by the time we were done, both Roger and Carrie had invited Christ into their hearts.

When I left, Carrie gave me a quick hug, and Roger thanked me. This time, the frown had been replaced by a smile.

Wow, Lord! I thought on the drive home. *That was awesome. I feel so encouraged. Thank You!*

Later, I heard that Roger was making amazing progress in his rehab. Carrie even invited me to come back to their house and pray again.

As the years went by, I thought more about what the Lord was teaching me about prayer. Of course He wanted me to pray for others. I knew that kind of prayer was effective. But there was something powerful about taking that extra step and praying in person. It changed the person with whom I prayed. It also changed me.

I tried to overcome my hesitation about praying with people. It slowly got a little easier. But ten years after that prayer time with Roger, the Lord sped up my training schedule.

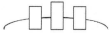

It was a couple of days after Christmas, and I was on vacation. I had enjoyed sledding with my kids during the afternoon. I was sleeping well that night—until about 3:00 a.m.

I woke with a start and knew immediately that it was the Lord. A vision filled my head. I saw the Elk River Library crowded with people. I recognized some as the pastors who met and prayed there every Tuesday. But there were many more.

I asked God, "Who are all these people?"

The Minnesota secretary of state, the mayor of Elk River, the superintendent of the Elk River school district.... The list went on. The Elk River police chief. The sheriff of Sherburne County. The Elk River director of parks and streets. The city director of finance. The high school principal.

Call them up, the Lord said. *Invite them to the library on a Tuesday at noon. Tell them exactly what I have said. When they come, sit them in a circle, lay hands on them, and pray for their needs. It is your responsibility to begin praying with your city. I want you to stop praying* for *the city and start praying* with *them.*

That was a message I had heard before. But who was I to call them up and ask them to pray? I didn't know most of these people. They would think I was nuts. And these were government and other public officials. My observation of people in public positions was that they usually avoided associations with religion at any cost.

I pictured Bruce Anderson, the county sheriff. He was a big man: six feet four inches, muscular, with a shaved head. I could imagine him intimidating even a hardened criminal. I was supposed to invite him to a prayer meeting?

Chuck, I will never send you to anyone who will rebuke My word as long as you give it in the moment of time I tell you to give it.

The Lord had spoken. And I realized I wouldn't be at peace until I obeyed.

Once I resolved to call, however, I came up with a strategy. God had told me that each one would accept the invitation. I couldn't imagine Bruce Anderson showing up at a prayer meeting, so I decided to call him first. If Bruce turned me down, it would mean I hadn't really heard from the Lord after all, and I wouldn't have to call anyone else.

From my office the next day, I looked up the number for the sheriff's department and punched it into my phone. As it turned out, Bruce wasn't in. But I reached one of his deputies and explained everything God had told me. I waited for him to say, "You've got to be kidding."

The response was far different, however. The deputy actually sounded excited about what I was saying. He promised to tell Bruce and seemed to think it would work out.

The deputy was so enthusiastic that I said, "Do you want to come, too?"

"Could I?" he said.

My strategy didn't seem to be working. But I didn't mind. God was up to something. I made more calls. To my amazement, every person on my list was available on the date I picked out, and everyone agreed to come. Now I was excited, too.

The Pray! Elk River prayer team, led by pastors Paul Salfrank of Alliance Community Church, Greg Pagh of Christ Lutheran Church, and Bob Pullar of the nondenominational Living Waters church, already met every Tuesday at the Elk River Library. About two weeks after my calls, our city and county representatives, along with the usual group of pastors and ministry and marketplace leaders, crowded into the library. Pastor Paul said, "OK, Chuck, you had the vision. What should we do?"

I explained how I had seen each representative sitting in a circle. The pastors and the rest of us were to stand in a circle around them, representing a covering of protection for the city. So that was what we did. Then our guests related their prayer requests, and we all prayed to the Lord for these petitions. I was amazed at the humble spirit revealed by each person that afternoon. Even Bruce Anderson, the burly sheriff, spoke in a soft voice, with his head down.

It was a wonderful time of fellowship. I left that afternoon with a strong sense of God's presence at the library and in our city.

Eight months later, that same group gathered again to see what had happened with our prayer requests and to praise God for the results. Tom Zerwas, the city police chief, reported that just two weeks after we prayed for a methamphetamine lab to be shut down, his department had made arrests that put the meth lab out of business. His other request, that four juveniles who were raising havoc throughout the city be stopped, came to pass within a month of our prayer gathering.

The Elk River mayor told us that a conflict between families in our city had been resolved. Bruce Anderson, who asked us to pray for peace and cooperation within his staff, reported that had happened. Every other city and county representative also had a testimony to offer.

God had clearly been at work. More incredible to me, however, was the transformation I was seeing within our city. Our leaders were developing an almost unheard-of openness to spiritual guidance and intervention.

The movement continued. Tom Zerwas retired as police chief and was replaced by a man named Jeff Beahen. I ran into Jeff in town and introduced myself.

"Chuck, say no more," he said. "I've heard all about you."

Uh-oh, I thought.

"I want to let you know that your prayers have protected our officers," Jeff said. "They've been fired upon, and I know that your prayers have made a difference. You are invited to come to my office anytime."

Since then, Jeff has attended several of our Tuesday meetings with the pastors to ask for prayer individually. Others have also approached me for individual prayer or just to talk—including Bruce Anderson, the sheriff I was so sure would turn me down.

Another new member of our group was Dr. Alan Jensen, who replaced David Flannery after David retired as superintendent of schools. Recently, the district hired yet another superintendent to replace Alan. The new superintendent is also planning to join our team for prayer. As other men and women come into the city and take leadership positions, they too are welcoming God's presence among us.

It is exciting for me to see God moving so clearly among the leadership of Elk River. We have only begun to tap into the potential of His love and power. If more cities throughout our nation and world will turn to God in this way, it will ignite a revival unlike anything we have seen before.

It can all begin with a prayer.

Most of us who call ourselves believers are willing to pray for another person in need. We know that God calls us to prayer, and we are comfortable doing that within the familiarity of our own homes. But Jesus gives us a much different picture of what prayer can look like. Though He certainly prayed alone, He spent much of His ministry traveling throughout the countryside, meeting with people and finding out about their needs. He listened to their troubles. He talked and ate with them. He placed His hands on them and prayed personally for their healing. There was nothing distant about Christ's ministry. He prayed *with* as many people as possible.

God desires for us to follow the example of His Son. People are deeply encouraged by active, in-person prayer. It leads to a renewed fellowship and builds their faith. And, as I have discovered many times, when we initiate prayer *with* others, we too are encouraged.

Prayer is powerful under any circumstances. But God does seem to reserve a special power and anointing for times when His followers meet in person to pray. Jesus said, "For where two or three come together in my name, there am I with them" (Matt. 18:20). That's a blessing I don't want to miss.

Chapter Four

JONAH

Principle #4: You can run, but you can't hide from God.

It was a spring day in 1998. I had been a mortgage loan officer with Marquette Bank, working in a region west of Minneapolis, for three years. I enjoyed modest success, but our family was still living paycheck to paycheck. When my appointment arrived at the bank near closing time, I wasn't especially eager to meet him. I had talked to Melvin on the phone a few times already. He was from Honduras, and I sometimes had trouble understanding his English. He had also been persistent, almost pushy, about scheduling a meeting with me.

"Good afternoon," Melvin said when he saw me. "I am here for my loan."

Melvin was a couple of inches shorter than me, stocky, with short black hair. I guessed he was in his early thirties. He wore a plaid shirt, jeans, and work boots.

We sat down and began going over the usual questions. But almost immediately, that familiar, inaudible voice interrupted my thoughts. It was the Lord.

Chuck, I want you to invite Melvin to a revival meeting.

Nearly every night for the past three weeks, I had been attending a revival meeting sponsored by an Elk River church at a local shopping mall. I had been going through a dry time spiritually, feeling distant from the Lord. Something about the worship and preaching at these gatherings was renewing me. The Word was real to me again, and my hunger for it returned. I was excited once again about my faith.

I didn't know why God wanted me to invite Melvin. He didn't seem like someone who would even consider going to a revival meeting. But I knew the Lord must have His reasons. *OK, Lord,* I thought. *I'll invite him when we're done here.*

We continued with the loan process. About twenty minutes later, I heard from the Lord again: *I want you to invite Melvin to a revival meeting.*

That was unusual. *I will, Lord,* I thought. *I'll invite him at the end of our meeting.*

We filled out more paperwork for Melvin's loan. He painted canvasses for a company that provided awnings for businesses. It sounded like hard work.

Finally, we were finished. As I gathered the papers on my desk into a folder, the Lord spoke to me a third time: *I want you to invite Melvin to a revival meeting.*

Now I was really surprised, and a little insulted. God had never told me three times to do anything. Did He think I needed this much reminding? *No,* I decided, *maybe it's that this is very important to the Lord. For some reason, He wants to be sure Melvin goes to this meeting.*

Melvin was standing up, ready to leave. I cleared my throat.

"Uh, Melvin, I've been going to these meetings lately," I said. "The Living Waters church is sponsoring them. They're revival meetings. I believe that you're supposed to come with me. Would you like to do that?"

I couldn't believe what happened next. This man just looked at me for a few moments. Then his eyes began tearing up.

Finally, he sat down and started to weep.

Through his tears, Melvin said, "Yes. Yes, I must come. I've been running from my father."

We talked, and more of Melvin's story came out. He hadn't seen his father, who still lived in Honduras, for nearly ten years. Melvin was ashamed to go to him. He had wasted many years on a wild life filled with drinking and drugs. He had neglected his father. He knew God wanted him to go back and make amends, but he just couldn't face him.

"Melvin," I said, "all I know is that you are very important to the Lord. He told me three times today to invite you to a revival meeting, and I've never heard Him do that before. You need to come to a meeting."

We shook hands, and Melvin agreed to join Kathi and me the next night.

The following evening, we met in the bank parking lot so Melvin could follow us to the revival meeting. Melvin introduced us to a young woman named Ivone and their two little children, Steven and Kimberly. The kids smiled shyly at us. At the time, I thought Ivone was Melvin's wife. Only later did I learn that they weren't married and that Melvin was separated, but not divorced, from his wife in Honduras.

At the revival meeting, I asked Bob Pullar, the Living Waters pastor, and Doug Stanton, the guest speaker, to pray personally for Melvin and Ivone. When they began praying, both Melvin and Ivone fell to the ground. The Holy Spirit was moving in them. Ivone stayed on the ground for about twenty minutes.

Melvin seemed nervous that night, but open to hearing from the Lord. He and Ivone kept coming back to the revival meetings. Soon Melvin was telling me, "Chuck, before, I never knew why I came to Minnesota. Now I know."

Melvin and Ivone began attending our church, and we all became good friends. As Kathi and I got to know them, we learned that they both had hearts for the Lord. We also found out that Ivone was in an uncomfortable situation. Though Melvin was a U.S. citizen, Ivone was not. She had already been caught once and deported after crossing a river from Mexico into the United States. She had successfully crossed the border on another attempt, so now she was living here illegally. She loved Melvin, but she lived in constant fear of being discovered and sent back to Mexico without him and her children.

About six months after our first meeting, after a church service, Melvin slipped away from Ivone and approached me. He looked troubled. I asked how he was doing.

"Something isn't right, Chuck," he said. "I'm not happy the way I used to be."

"Things have changed for you," I said. "God's grace has lifted." I don't think Melvin understood what I meant, but we didn't have time to discuss it further.

Later, I thought and prayed about Melvin's words. I realized that God was moving in his life, and He wanted me, as Melvin's friend, to help Melvin take the next step. I discussed the matter with Paul Salfrank, our pastor, and he agreed that the time was right for Kathi and me to talk with Melvin and Ivone.

I wasn't looking forward to it, but I knew it had to be done.

A couple of weeks later, on a Sunday after church, Kathi and I invited Melvin and Ivone over to our home in Elk River. Kathi served cookies and lemonade. Melvin and Ivone sat on our rattan couch in the living room, Kathi was in a chair next to them, and I squatted on the floor.

After we chatted for a few minutes, I took a deep breath and plunged in.

"Melvin, you mentioned to me a while back that you don't feel happy," I said. "I need to share with you the reason you're not happy: grace has lifted. The Lord is allowing you to start seeing the sin in your life. You need to make a change.

"I know you're still legally married. You have two choices. You need to either go back and make things right with your wife in Honduras and release Ivone so that she can find a husband, or you need to go through the legal process, divorce your wife in Honduras, and marry Ivone so that she can become a U.S. citizen. This situation isn't fair to Ivone. She's living in fear. And you're not fulfilling your responsibility as the father of your children."

I watched the frown on Melvin's face deepen, but I kept going.

"Melvin, I'm not going to tell you which choice to make. You need to ask the Lord about that. But—"

"What if the Lord doesn't want me to do either?" Melvin said.

I stifled a laugh. "Melvin, that's not an option. I'm certain the Lord wants you to make one of these choices. Doing nothing is not a choice."

Melvin scowled, but he allowed me to pray that God would give him a revelation about what he should do. He and Ivone left our home soon after.

I didn't see Melvin for the next three months. He didn't come to church. He didn't call. He didn't stop in at the bank. It was as if he had disappeared.

I was driving home from work one evening and praying. "Lord," I said, "what's going on with Melvin? I don't see him anymore."

He's like Jonah, the Lord said. I knew whom He was talking about—the Old Testament figure that ran away when God called him to Nineveh. *Melvin can run, but he can't hide. He'll be back.*

A couple of weeks later, Kathi and I attended a Sunday brunch in our church basement. We finished eating and were taking our plates to the church kitchen when I spotted a man scanning the crowd. It was Melvin.

He saw me and hurried over.

"Chuck," he said, "I need to talk to you and Pastor Paul. Do you have a few minutes?"

We found Paul and went upstairs to his office. And soon as we sat down, the words came pouring out.

"OK," Melvin said. His eyes were brimming with tears. "OK. I'll do it. I don't know what else to do. I am so unhappy with my life right now. I'll do it."

I felt I knew what he meant, but I needed to be certain. "Melvin, the Lord told me that you're like Jonah, that you can run, but you can't hide," I said. "You've got to stop running. Are you willing to do what you need to do to make things right?"

"Yes," he said. "Yes."

A few weeks later, a friend and I decided to go to Honduras to attend a Christian crusade there. We invited Melvin to join us, and he accepted. It was his chance to restore his relationship with his father and with the Lord.

When we arrived in Honduras, Melvin called his wife and told her that he wanted to make their separation legal with a divorce. She had no objection—they hadn't spoken to each other for years. She agreed to sign the necessary papers.

Then, during one of the last days of our visit, came Melvin's toughest task.

Two friends from the crusade and I joined Melvin on the drive into the Honduras countryside. The dirt road, filled with potholes, rose and fell like waves on the ocean. We passed house after house protected by barbed wire. The farther we drove, the smaller the houses got.

It was near dusk when we arrived at a tiny, white stucco house. This was the home of Melvin's wife, Olivia, whom we met as we entered the house, along with his father, Rodrigo.

We helped them finish preparations for a tamale and rice dinner. The conversation was in Spanish, so I didn't understand most of it. But I could tell it was an emotional reunion by the way everyone talked at once, the intensity of their expressions, and the way Rodrigo's eyes glistened.

After dinner, we asked Rodrigo if we could pray for him. He knelt down in the small living room. The rest of us stood in a circle around him to bless and pray for him.

Then Melvin said something, and the room turned absolutely still. Melvin approached Rodrigo and dropped to his knees so that his knees touched his father's. Melvin put his head down and in a quiet voice began to speak. I still didn't understand the specific words, but I knew what he was saying. Melvin was repenting for being a rebellious son. He was asking for his father's forgiveness. The prodigal son had come home.

When Melvin finished speaking, I held my breath. Then Rodrigo reached out with both arms and folded Melvin into a long, tear-filled embrace. Melvin was forgiven.

My friends and I praised God for what we were witnessing. It was an unforgettable scene.

Our group returned to Minnesota. As the months passed, Melvin continued to fill out the proper forms to make his divorce official. Nearly a year after he started, the process was finally almost finished. All that remained was for a judge to approve the documents.

I was at work in the spring of 2001 when I received a call from Melvin. "Chuck, guess what?" he said. "I need you and Kathi to come down today and be our witnesses in court, be our best man and matron of honor." The deadline for a federal amnesty program for illegal aliens expired that day. If Melvin could get his divorce approved that morning and marry Ivone in the afternoon, she would qualify for the amnesty program and be pronounced a U.S. citizen.

God was watching out for Melvin. The Sherburne County judge was married to a woman from South America, and he knew how much it would mean to Melvin and Ivone to qualify for the amnesty. That afternoon, Kathi and I stood behind Ivone and Melvin as they said their "I dos" before the judge. Ivone beamed. At last, she and Melvin were married.

Melvin seemed a changed man. A few weeks before the wedding, he asked about using our church for worship services. He had been mentoring and ministering to members of his family and others in the Hispanic community, and they needed a place to meet. But he wanted to serve the Lord even more directly. He wanted to become a pastor.

That started conversations between Melvin and me, our church leadership team, and other pastors in the city. We all saw what God was doing with Melvin, and we wanted to encourage him however we could. Our church agreed to let Melvin hold his meetings there. And we agreed to help him pursue his new dream.

Four years later, that dream came true. In addition to being a devoted husband and father, Melvin is now a licensed and ordained pastor in Elk River. His congregation has grown from the fifteen people who attended those first meetings to nearly a hundred. They continue to meet and worship in our church. His ministry is called *luz de Cristo*—"Light of Christ"—and brings much hope and spiritual guidance to our Hispanic community.

Today, Melvin sometimes joins me in speaking at events. When I introduce him, I say that it is a miracle he is with me. He was a man on the run from his responsibilities and his earthly father. He was also—like Jonah—running from his spiritual Father.

Melvin isn't running anymore. He has found his home.

When the Lord told Jonah, "Go to the great city of Nineveh and preach against it, because its wickedness has come up before me" (Jon. 1:2), Jonah headed in the opposite direction. He boarded a ship bound for Tarshish, a port more than a thousand miles away. But there is no place on Earth that God does not see. The Lord created a storm that raged until Jonah was thrown into the sea and swallowed by a great fish. There, Jonah finally submitted to the will of God, praying, "When my life was ebbing away, I remembered you, Lord, and my prayer rose to you, to your holy temple" (Jon. 2:7). Jonah then escaped to dry land. This time, when God told him to go to Nineveh, Jonah went.

So often, when the Lord asks us to do something we don't want to do, we try to fool Him. We think we can outrun or hide from Him. But it never works. Sooner or later, we end up with more trouble than we started with. And relief doesn't come until we submit to the Lord.

I've learned that lesson many times in my life. Melvin discovered the same truth, and he's much happier now that he's following the path the Lord has laid before him. The next time God calls on you, I suggest that you follow His lead. You'll save yourself a lot of trouble.

Chapter Five

FREEDOM

Principle #5: Forgiveness will set you free.

I am on the road a lot, and over the years I have seen more than a few drivers suddenly speed up and pass me easily. In seconds, their vehicles jumped from going the speed limit to going ninety miles an hour. They had a feature that car salesmen love to brag about: *acceleration.*

On my drive to work one morning, however, the Lord spoke to me about a different kind of acceleration—one that seemed just as exciting and dangerous.

I was twenty-seven years old and still a salesman at a Levitz furniture store. The thirty-mile commute from my home in Osseo to the store in St. Paul was usually uneventful, but on this morning the Lord interrupted my thoughts.

Chuck, He said, *when you turn forty, I'm going to begin to use you. I've been using you, but I'm going to accelerate things in your life.*

"Yes, Lord," I answered. But even as I said this, I couldn't help thinking that others would do a better job. "Lord, why do You keep doing this, speaking to me this way? I don't even go to church on a regular basis. Aren't there a lot of other people that You could work with?"

I have chosen you, He said.

I still didn't understand, but the matter was settled for now.

The issue of acceleration didn't come up again for another thirteen years. In December 1998, I was thirty-nine years old. I was doing well as a mortgage loan officer. I had also come out of a dry time spiritually and was feeling a renewed hunger for God. I had been attending revival meetings in the area nearly every night.

After one of those meetings, I was at home in my backyard, gazing at the stars and thinking about the day, when the Lord suddenly resumed the conversation He began so long before.

Chuck, remember what you said yes to thirteen years ago?

I knew immediately what He meant. I hadn't forgotten. But I was just starting to refocus on the Lord again. I did not feel like a very good candidate to be used for any acceleration plan. I was still trying to get back to where I was in my Christian walk several years before. And so, like Moses on Mount Horeb, I had the audacity to argue with God's choice.

"No, Lord," I said. "You can't use me. Look at my life. It would be easy for You. There are so many people out there who could serve You better. Go find someone else. I don't know anything."

Perfect, He said. *Less that I have to correct. Since you don't know anything, you don't know what you "can't" say or "can't" do. I can use somebody like that. I have chosen you.*

I should have known better than to think I could win an argument with God. He wins every time. But sometimes I need a lot of convincing. So I resorted to the real reason why I would make a poor servant—the reason I was sure He was making a mistake.

"Lord, You know what?" I said. My words came out more slowly. I didn't want to say them. "I know that You have forgiven me. But I haven't forgiven myself. Every time I come to worship You, the enemy reminds me of my past, of all the sin in my life. Lord, it is just too hard."

There. It was out in the open. I admitted it. I wasn't good enough to serve Him. I felt completely inadequate and unworthy.

I somehow expected the Lord to walk away and find someone else to carry on His work. But He didn't. Instead, it was as if a loving father gently pulled me onto his lap and put his arm around me to offer an encouraging hug.

Chuck, the Lord said, *I'm going to teach you how to forgive yourself. What I want you to do is go on a forty-day juice fast. I guarantee that you will not hunger for anything other than Me.*

I had never fasted in my life. I heard about people doing it and read about in Scripture, but I never paid much attention.

"When?" I asked.

January 1, 1999.

The next morning, I pulled out a calendar and counted out the days. If I started fasting on January 1, the forty days would end on February 9. My fortieth birthday would be on February 10, 1999.

It didn't take me long to start praying again. "OK, Lord, you've got my attention," I said. "But why are You doing this?"

His answer blew me away. It began with a vision of a man running on a dusty road near a mountaintop. The man disappeared around a bend.

Chuck, I have chosen you as a forerunner, the Lord said. *I am going to take you places where people can't see. I am going to show you things in the future and have you tell people what I've shown you so that they will be prepared. A runner cannot run a straight race if he always has his head turned to look behind. The sin in your past is like baggage. It's weighing you down. I am going to sever that sin so I can accelerate the things in your life.*

I don't want you to look where you've been. I want you to turn around and look where I want you to go. Don't look to your past. Look to your future.

Now I was starting to get excited. This was sounding pretty good after all. "Lord, how are You going to do this?"

The forty days of your fast will represent forty years of your life. Each day will represent one year. Every morning you will get up, take a shower, and do a prophetic act. You will stand before Me and wash yourself physically; at the same moment, I am going to wash away the sin from that year of your life. The first years of life are grace, but then enter the years of accountability.

During your fast, I want you to go to certain people and ask for their forgiveness. There are things you've stolen, done, or spoken. These people may not know that you've sinned against them. But I don't care if it was done twenty days ago or twenty years ago; I want you to go back and ask for forgiveness. It's not only for you. It's also for them.

I told Kathi about my incredible conversations with the Lord and His instruction to fast. Her first response wasn't entirely encouraging: "Chuck, you're nuts. You're going to die."

"No, I'm not," I said. "The Lord told me I can do this."

Others warned me that I needed to ease into such a lengthy fast. They said I should gradually cut down on eating so my body would have time to adjust to no food at all. But I didn't worry about that. The Lord had told me what to do.

From the first day of the fast, I didn't suffer from any pain or terrible hunger. In fact, I enjoyed it. Just as the Lord had said, I found myself wanting to read and bask in His Word more than ever. I could only describe what I was doing as a "supernatural fast."

Each day I woke up, stepped into the shower, and tried to recall the year of my life that day represented. The first few mornings were easy. It was exactly as God had told me. There was grace during my early years, so there was nothing to be forgiven for.

At the end of that first week, though, a memory from when I was seven years old came to me. I was walking by a park a few blocks from my home and saw a big delivery truck parked there. It was white, with a huge wooden sign on both sides that covered up half of the truck's back tires. A string of yellow lights ran all the way around the sign. The whole thing looked like something out of a carnival.

I looked around; no one was watching. I knew it wasn't right, but I had the urge to break something. It was just an old truck. Who would care?

I walked up and started kicking the light bulbs, smashing them one by one. The shattered remains left a trail around the truck.

But I wasn't alone after all. A man approached. "Hey, kid!" he shouted. "Stop that!"

I ran home as fast as I could and hid under my bed. But the man followed me. Soon he was telling my dad what happened. The result was an unpleasant spanking.

Standing in the shower all those years later, I knew I was responsible for what I did that day. I had entered my period of accountability.

"Lord," I prayed, "I ask You to forgive me for breaking those lights. Please also forgive me for running away and for doing what I knew was wrong."

Immediately, I experienced such a cleansing wash over me. It was as if a weight I'd been carrying for years had suddenly been removed. It was a great way to start the day.

My fast continued. There were mornings where I sensed the Lord telling me to go to a specific person and ask for forgiveness. Those days were the hardest, because I didn't want to admit what I had done. But after I confessed to someone, I enjoyed the most glorious evenings, because in each case the burden of my sin, often after many years, had lifted.

On some days, I was reminded of difficult moments with my parents—all the arguing, fighting, and drinking. I asked for God's forgiveness for things I had said and done to them. I also saw how I held on to anger against my parents for all this time. I asked the Lord to forgive me for not forgiving them. Each time, it was as if a brick was taken away.

God was teaching me much about forgiveness. And as I learned, the walls surrounding me kept falling down. I hadn't even realized that I was imprisoned by my bitterness and sin.

Now I was free.

It was day thirty-six, while I was worshiping in church during a conference, that the Lord gave me a vision. In His hand I saw three large, gold keys.

"Lord, what do these keys represent?" I said.

They represent the marketplace, the government, and the church. I am going to give you favor in all three of these areas. No door will be locked to you.

Only years later would I understand what God meant by this statement. He planned to open doors for me to places I would never have imagined. For now, I tucked away the image of the keys in my mind.

Soon the end of my fast, and my fortieth birthday, approached. It had been an incredible experience. But I had a question for God.

"Lord, I'm confused," I prayed, "You said every day of my fast is for my past. But my fortieth year, on day forty, I haven't lived yet. That's my future. What do You want me to do on that last day?"

Chuck, I want you to give up everything for the last day of your fast, He said. *No juice. No water. Absolutely nothing.*

"Why is that, Lord?"

It will be a prophetic act. This is what I'm going to ask you to do for the rest of your life. I'm going to ask you to die to yourself and give up everything for Me.

I was excited. I couldn't wait. But Kathi still worried about me. This time she really thought I was going to die. In the middle of the night before that final day of my fast, she got up and prayed for my health and for God's hand to be on me.

While she prayed, I slept like a baby.

That last day felt like a blessing. I had no desire to eat or drink. Instead, I spent the hours praying, reading my Bible, and reflecting on what I had learned over the past forty days. God was so good to me.

I didn't want the fast to end. A few days earlier, I prayed, "Lord, do I have to go back to eating? It's more enjoyable not eating."

Grace will lift, He said.

February 10 was my fortieth birthday and the end of the fast. And grace did lift. All of a sudden, I was ravenously hungry. I waited until noon to celebrate, and then I went right back to my normal diet: hamburgers, soup, even birthday cake. People told me later that was dangerous, that the sudden change could have completely disrupted my digestive system. But I never had any problems. God took care of me.

Since then, I have tried to apply what I learned about forgiveness to my life. I realized something had changed almost two years to the day after the end of my fast. Kathi and I, and all five kids, had enjoyed a relaxing weekend vacation at a hotel in Duluth, Minnesota, off of Lake Superior. We arrived on a Friday night and watched nearly ten inches of snow turn the city into a winter wonderland.

All too soon it was Sunday morning and time to head home. Our suitcases were packed and waiting by the door of our suite. But first, Kathi and I wanted to have "church." We gathered the family around the kitchen table, where I read from Scripture. Then the Holy Spirit moved Kathi and me to address our children.

"You know, your mom and I would like to pray a blessing over each of you," I said, darting a glance at Kathi. "But we've come to realize as parents that we have not honored our kids properly. We want to come to you this morning and repent to you."

Starting with Tanner, who was twenty-one at the time, I apologized for mistakes I made as a father. "Tanner, I know I have not always done the best job with you. There are things I've said that I shouldn't have. There are things I haven't said—how much I love you, and how proud I am of you. I probably spanked you too hard when I was angry. I need to repent and ask for God's forgiveness and for your forgiveness."

Kathi did the same thing, repenting to Tanner and asking for his and the Lord's forgiveness. Then we invited our children, if they wanted, to also repent to Tanner. Before we knew it, each family member was repenting to the other. Then Kathi and I prayed a blessing for each child, and our kids blessed each other. But the best part was when, after Kathi and I finished our blessings, our kids looked at each other, then stood one by one and began repenting to and blessing us.

It was a wonderful, emotional time that went on for an hour and a half. There were so many tears that we had to pull out a roll of toilet paper to dry everyone's eyes. By the end, I was emotionally drained—and happy.

Lord, You can take me home anytime, I thought. *We've experienced so much healing today. I feel so blessed and honored.*

There have been other amazing days since my fast. The Lord has been true to His word. My life, spiritually and otherwise, has accelerated in astonishing ways. There are times when it can feel a little overwhelming, like riding a roller coaster that only goes faster and never stops. But I am at peace about it all.

One reason is that, since the forty-day fast, I begin each day the same way. As I cleanse myself in the shower, I pray, "Lord, please forgive me if I offended or dishonored You yesterday." And I immediately sense His forgiveness. By repenting daily, I never have to look back further than twenty-four hours. I begin each day renewed, refreshed, and free of the baggage of past sin.

Today, as I run my race for Him, I keep my head pointed straight ahead. I am looking toward the future, and I can't wait.

People often ask me how I can hear God's voice so clearly. I don't fully understand it myself. I can't explain why the Lord has blessed me this way. But I do believe one of the reasons may be that I don't allow sin to become an obstacle to hearing Him speak. By seeking and receiving His forgiveness daily for every one of my sins—and then by forgiving myself—there is nothing to block or distract me from listening to His will for my life.

The act of repentance is important to the Lord. He knows how an unforgiven or unforgiving heart can be torn apart from the inside. God stands ready to forgive and forget any of our mistakes if we will only ask Him in a spirit of humility. He expects us to do the same. While it's not always easy to forgive someone else for hurting you, the hardest person to forgive may be yourself.

If you are struggling as I did to forgive yourself for past sins, I encourage you to follow the instruction of Scripture: "Forgive as the Lord forgave you" (Col. 3:13). You will leave behind chains you didn't know you had and enter a new life of liberty.

Chapter Six

DIVINE APPOINTMENT

*Principle #6: Be ready. Your next appointment
may be a divine appointment.*

On a busy day in my work as a mortgage loan officer, I might see three customers in my office and take another twenty business calls. Some people will drop in to apply for a loan. Most call to make an appointment.

But there are meetings scheduled by man, and there are meetings scheduled by God. The former are simply business transactions. The latter are what I call divine appointments—and I rarely know beforehand when the Lord is setting the agenda.

Randy was my first appointment one hot August morning in Elk River. He arrived at 8:30 and plopped into the burgundy club chair across from my desk. He wore a gray polo shirt and tan Dockers. I also noticed something else—a weariness in his eyes, as if he'd been dragging around an invisible ball and chain for far too long.

After we exchanged greetings, he surprised me by apologizing. "Chuck, I'm sorry. I'm kind of out of it. I had to take some pain medication this morning. I have severe back pain."

Randy explained more about his condition. As he talked, I heard the voice of the Lord: *I want you to pray with him for healing.*

I put down the pen in my hand. *OK, Lord, here we go,* I thought. At that point, I knew that my meeting with Randy was going to involve more than a loan application.

"Randy," I said, "it sounds like this back problem has been a real issue for you. I'd like to offer to pray with you for healing. Could we do that?"

I'm sure Randy hadn't expected to hear those words from a loan officer, but he didn't object. "That would be fine," he said.

I began to pray. In the name of Jesus, I commanded the infirmity that had plagued Randy to leave his body. I asked the Lord to heal him. I asked for a sense of peace to come over his body, mind, heart, and spirit.

As I prayed, I saw Randy's eyes well up with tears. I don't think anyone had ever prayed like this with him before.

"Randy," I said when I finished, "have you ever prayed to invite Jesus Christ into your life?"

"No, I haven't."

"Would you like to do that now?"

He blinked his eyes and nodded. "Yes. Yes, I would."

We prayed, and Randy was even more moved than before. In just our first few minutes together, we had prayed for his healing and salvation. It was as if pressure that had built up for years had now been released. A dam had broken.

For the next hour, while I typed up Randy's loan application, he poured out the story of his family to me. He told me about family problems that ranged from legal trouble to marital disunity.

I understood why God had me pray so quickly with Randy. He wanted me to have time to hear about the troubles weighing on Randy's heart.

At my suggestion, we prayed again, this time for Randy's family. After I prayed, I opened my eyes and said, "Randy, the Lord just spoke to me. He told me your wife has been praying for you for many years. When you leave my office, you are supposed to call her and tell her that her prayers for her husband have been answered today. Also, even though your children are now in their thirties, you need to go home and repent to them for not being the spiritual leader of your home."

Those were bold words. I had never said anything like that to someone before. Yet I sensed it was God's response to one of my frequent prayers: "Lord, never let anything come out of my mouth before its time. But never let anything stay in my mouth that needs to come out."

I wasn't sure how Randy would react. I feared he might be angry with me. But he wasn't. He only nodded his head and said in a low voice, "Yes, I'll do that."

He was humbled by a message from the Lord.

Randy and I said our good-byes. When we shook hands, he gripped my hand tightly and held on for a moment. Then he was gone.

About forty-five minutes later, my phone rang. The woman on the line was weeping. It was Randy's wife, Marilyn.

"Randy told me what happened," she said. "I want you to know that I have been praying for my husband for years. I just want to say thank you for what happened in your office today."

"There's no need to thank me," I said. "You're the one who's been praying. I just did what God told me to do."

The next day I received another phone call. It was Randy's son.

"I want to thank you so much for what you did for my father," he said.

"What do you mean?"

The son told me what had happened the night before. When Randy arrived home from our appointment, he gathered together the family members that were in the house—his wife, son, and grandchildren—in the kitchen. After they all sat down, Randy began speaking in a halting voice.

"I just want to tell you guys that I...I need to repent," he said. "I have not been the spiritual leader of this family that I should have been."

With those words out, he began to weep.

I was moved to hear how God had intervened in this family.

Several months passed. I hadn't heard much about Randy and his family for some time. I was working in my office when Randy's face suddenly came to mind. *I wonder how they're doing?* I thought.

Not long after, Marilyn called. "Chuck, you don't know it, but my husband has been diagnosed with cancer," she said. "We're at the hospital now. My pastor just left, but Randy is asking for you. When you prayed with him, something happened to his life. No one's ever moved him like you did. Would you pray with him again?"

I had never visited a customer at the hospital before. But soon I was walking down the corridor and into Randy's hospital room, greeting him and Marilyn.

I could see that Randy was weak, but he was sitting up in bed. An IV machine was hooked to his arm. We talked for several minutes. Then I prayed for peace, for comfort, and for any healing that would be within God's will.

About two weeks later, Marilyn asked me to visit again. By this time, Randy had been transferred to another hospital. The doctors said he had only a few days to live.

When I arrived, I noticed immediately that Randy was weaker than before. He was lying down this time. But he was still happy to see me.

We talked about everything that had happened during the past few months, including the amazing reconciliation Randy had enjoyed with the rest of his family. Then we held hands as I prayed once again. Randy held on to my hand after I was done.

"Chuck, I want you to know that I did all these things before I knew I had cancer. Thank you so much for talking and praying with me so I was able to have that time with my family."

"Randy," I said, squeezing his hand, "would you do one favor for me? When you get to heaven, would you give Jesus a big hug for me?"

"Absolutely," he said.

On my drive home, I reflected on what had just happened. I grieved for Randy's family, of course. They were about to lose a husband, father, and grandfather. But I thanked God that this repentant man had been able to see so many wonderful changes in his family at the end of his life. Best of all, I thanked Him that Randy could look forward to a new and eternal home.

Soon, Randy would be meeting Jesus face-to-face. I wished I could be there to see it. *That,* I thought with a smile, *will truly be a divine appointment.*

I believe that God schedules divine appointments for each of us every day. They are opportunities He gives us to serve Him and the body of Christ. Unfortunately, too many of us don't keep those appointments. We have lots of excuses: We're comfortable where we are. We'd rather mind our own business. We don't want to push our religion on someone else.

When we miss a divine appointment, we waste a chance to help someone else. But we also miss out on a wonderful blessing for ourselves. When I obey God's direction and intervene in someone's life—when I choose to be used—I experience one of the great rewards in life. There is nothing like the feeling that comes from seeing God transform lives and families. Somehow, their newfound joy gets reflected back to me. Once it happens, I can't wait for God to use me again.

If you want more fulfillment and joy in your life, watch for your next divine appointment. It's one meeting you won't want to miss.

Chapter Seven

A PROMISE KEPT

Principle #7: Hold on to God's promises.

My sister Debbie is three years older than me. She is a friendly, outgoing woman who thinks of others before herself. I love her dearly, and I know she loves me—though I couldn't really blame her if she didn't. You see, while growing up, my brothers and I weren't always very nice to Debbie.

Let's just say we were mischievous.

As the oldest child, Debbie was often stuck babysitting the rest of us while my dad and mom were at work or a bar. That meant she had to keep track of three energetic boys and an outgoing baby sister named June. It wasn't an easy task.

One summer day when she was about fifteen, my parents were gone and Debbie was trying to get my brothers and me to help her clean the kitchen. We weren't even slightly interested. To make sure Debbie got the message, my older brother, Dan, was mouthing off. "You can't make me do it," he said. "I don't want to, and I don't have to." My younger brother, Russell, and I chimed in when we could think of a good line to add.

Finally, Debbie had heard enough. She grabbed a broom and used it as a weapon, waving it around wildly and poking us with the handle.

"You guys never listen to me!" she yelled. "I'm telling Mom and Papa!"

We dove under the kitchen table and evaded her stabs by hiding behind the chairs. That only made Debbie madder. She swung and poked even harder.

You need to know that our house had no air conditioning, so the windows were always open in the summer. Most of the window screens had holes in them; some windows didn't have screens at all. The result was that our home was frequently infested with flies.

My father's solution to this problem was to hang fly catchers from the ceiling all over the house. These were the old kind—a strip of tape covered with a brown, smelly, syrupy goop that attracted and trapped little insect feet. Of course, we rarely replaced the fly catchers, so it didn't take long for each one to be covered with what looked like more than a hundred dead or dying fly carcasses.

Two of these disgusting contraptions were hanging from the kitchen ceiling the day we cowered under the kitchen table.

You can probably guess what happened. As we dodged and weaved on our knees, Debbie reared back for a mighty swing and raised her broom just a little too high. It caught one of the fly catchers and knocked it loose. To the surprise of all of us, the device—brown goop, dead flies, and all—landed squarely on her head and stuck there.

Debbie screamed. Then she burst into tears and ran out of the house, grabbing frantically at her hair. My brothers and I laughed so hard that we couldn't get up. When our family gets together and we talk about that story now, Deb laughs with us. But it took a while for her to see the humor in it.

It was another summer almost three decades later when I visited Deb at her home in Melrose. By this point we got along great. She was married, had three kids, and worked as a real estate agent.

Deb was a good Catholic. She attended Mass every Sunday. But as far as I could tell, she didn't have a personal relationship with the Lord. And that bothered me.

Starting with my mom eighteen years earlier, I had led every other member of my immediate family to Jesus—my parents, my brothers and younger sister, and my children, as well as my eighty-five-year-old grandmother. In each case, the Lord had showed me when a family member was open to talking and praying about salvation.

All except Deb.

I took a walk by myself in Deb's yard. I recalled the promise the Lord had made to me the night I prayed with my mom in her final days at the hospital: *Chuck, because of your obedience, I promise you I will give you all of your family.*

"Lord, it's been eighteen years," I prayed. "When are you going to give me my sister?"

The Lord may not have responded that day, but He heard me well enough. His answer began taking shape about three months later in an unexpected way.

Deb's son Adam was taking religion classes at St. Mary's Catholic School in Melrose—the same school that I had gone to as a boy. Now he was taking a confirmation class, and the instructor asked Deb if my brother Dan and I would be willing to speak at one of Adam's classes. The teacher knew we had both attended St. Mary's. He also knew about our problems with drugs as teens and that we had moved on to better things. He thought we might be a positive example for the class.

Dan didn't like giving speeches, so he declined the invitation. Though I enjoyed telling stories, I had hardly spoken in public myself and was nervous about the idea. I asked God if I should go.

Yes, He said. *I want you to pray that they will have an intimate relationship with Me. If you do this, I promise you at least thirteen children will come to know Me.*

And so, on a snowy day in November, I found myself driving Kathi and my daughter Amber to Melrose. The last time I had set foot in St. Mary's was my final day of school in sixth grade, probably the same year as the fly catcher incident. It was strange to be back. Everything was exactly the same—the pebbled flooring, the green panels on the wall. When I walked into the gym, I noticed everything there also looked the same as in my youth, only much smaller. Had it really been almost thirty years since I studied and played here?

The crowd filtered in and began taking their seats in the metal chairs that covered the gym floor. I hadn't prepared a speech, so I asked the instructor if I needed to talk about anything specific.

"Talk about your life or anything you want," he said. "We've given you an hour."

Soon I was at the front of the room addressing sixty kids and their families. For the first few minutes, I related all the terrible things from my early life—the drinking, the drugs, and my father's violent temper. I was really getting into it.

Suddenly I heard the Lord speaking to me: *That's enough credit for Satan. I want the rest of the time. Tell them how good your life is now.*

I paused to gather my thoughts. Then, just as God instructed, I spoke about what had changed, how I now had a personal relationship with Jesus Christ, and how blessed I was that He was speaking to me and directing me. Then I invited everyone present to join me in the salvation prayer and invite Jesus into their lives. I closed my eyes and prayed.

After I finished, I asked those who prayed with me to raise their hands. Thirteen kids—exactly as the Lord had said—put their arms in the air. That didn't surprise me. But what left me stunned were the four adult hands in the air. One of them was the instructor's.

Another was Deb's.

She smiled at me. I grinned back.

Yes, Lord! I thought. *This is so awesome. Thank You for fulfilling Your promise from eighteen years ago and giving me my sister. And please forgive me for complaining. Your timing is always best.*

Now each of my brothers and sisters, along with my parents and kids, are part of God's eternal family. No matter what happened during the rest of our lives on earth, we could all look forward to a joyful reunion in heaven.

But the Lord wasn't done. He didn't just keep His promise to me. His blessing a few years later, in the midst of a terrible loss, went beyond what He promised or what I expected.

In 1991, I had led my father to the Lord one evening in my car after picking him up at an alcohol treatment center. It was the first time we had prayed together. After that night, though, we prayed together many times. We grew closer as the years passed, and he became very open to the idea of prayer.

Sometimes my dad would share that he wasn't feeling well physically or that he was having a financial problem. I would say, "Papa, can we pray about that?" He would answer, "Yeah, let's do that. You go ahead." He would close his eyes and agree with everything I prayed. For much of my life, I couldn't even have imagined praying with my dad. I was grateful for these moments.

It was a gray December day in 2004 when Deb went to visit my father at his home in Melrose. She was a faithful, loving daughter and often stopped by to see how he was doing. My dad never locked his door when he was home, so when no one answered the door that day, Deb let herself in.

She found him on the kitchen floor. He had suffered either a heart attack or a stroke. At age seventy-four, Joseph Ripka was dead.

Kathi and I had taken Papa out to dinner just two weeks earlier. He seemed tired then, but in good spirits. Now, just like that, he was gone. I could hardly believe it.

The next few days were spent talking with my brothers and sisters and working on funeral preparations.

I was in my office at work when I remembered another promise the Lord had made to me: *I will bring light to darkness even in times of death.* I thought about those words and shook my head. I was grateful that my dad was in heaven, but my heart was still heavy. I missed him. At that moment, I couldn't see any light at all.

"Lord," I prayed, "how will you bring light to the darkness of my father's death?"

He answered me: *I want you to give the salvation message at your father's funeral.*

As always, I wanted to be obedient. But the funeral would be at St. Mary's Catholic Church. Offering the salvation prayer at a funeral was something people just did not do. Would I be bringing light or creating dissension?

Still, I supposed the Lord knew what He was doing. He was still God, after all. Whether it made sense or not, I needed to trust Him.

"Lord," I finally said, "I don't feel that I should just announce to my family that I'm going to speak at the funeral. If You want me to speak, You need to open the door."

The next day, I met my brothers and sisters at St. Mary's to make the final funeral arrangements. The church representative who was helping us asked if anyone would be willing to say a few words at the service.

Deb turned to me. "Chuckie, you enjoy speaking. Why don't you get up and speak at Papa's funeral?"

The door was open.

And so, a few days later, I stood at a podium before more than one hundred fifty of my parents' family and friends inside the century-old church in Melrose. I took in the high, arched ceiling, as well as the ornate statues of Jesus, Joseph, Mary, and others inlaid with gold. I was nervous. *Lord, how are we going to do this?* I thought. *I've never done anything like this before.*

Before the service, I asked the priest, a sixty-something man wearing a red sash over his traditional robes, if I could tell a story about my mom and dad. He agreed.

So I talked about my parents. I told how I had prayed with each of them and showed them how to invite Jesus into their lives so they could spend eternity in heaven.

I took a moment to let my eyes roam over the faces in the crowd. "My dad is now in heaven with my mom," I said. "I know they would like each of you to one day join them in eternity. Now I'm going to say the same prayer that I prayed with Mom and Papa. I'm going to pray this out loud, and I'd like to invite you to join me."

As I prayed, I glanced up. It appeared that everyone there was praying with me.

I looked at my extended family—aunts, uncles, cousins, and more. I looked at my brothers and sisters. I looked at Deb, the final piece in God's promise, whom I'd prayed about for so many years. We were all part of the same family—God's family. And we were all going to be enjoying each other's company for a very long time.

The Lord's perspective is very different from ours. What may seem a long time to us—such as the eighteen years I waited for the Lord to deliver each member of my family into His kingdom—is a barely noticeable tick of the clock for the Creator of the universe. As you wait for God to fulfill His promises to you, you may become disheartened. You may even get so discouraged that you lose faith and throw those promises away.

More than once, when I felt I couldn't wait a moment longer, I prayed for the Lord to keep a promise to me and then watched it come to pass. Once I pressed Him for an explanation: "Lord, why do I have to remind You of Your promises?"

You don't have to remind Me, He said. *I was testing you. When you brought it back to Me, I knew you believed it.*

I urge you to hold on to the Lord's promises. Our Father is "the faithful God, keeping his covenant of love to a thousand generations of those who love him and keep his commands" (Deut. 7:9). He will never go back on a promise. His Word stands true for all eternity.

Don't discard His promises when He doesn't answer according to your timetable. Wait patiently instead. When you trust in His ways and in His timing, you will never be disappointed.

Chapter Eight

TAKING BACK THE SCHOOLS

*Principle #8: Spiritual battles
are won through prayer.*

L ike a black, roiling storm cloud that never goes away, a spirit of despair and death hung over the Elk River School District during the 1999–2000 school year. It arrived on September 1, the very first day of school. There was an assembly for the students at Elk River High School, as well as a picnic where sodas, apples, and cookies were served.

A seemingly happy sixteen-year-old student was among the student body that first day. It turned out to be his last day. He went home that afternoon and killed himself.

Later that month, the principal of the Elk River alternative high school for troubled teens died in what was ruled a suicide. Over Christmas break, a student died from leukemia. In January, another Elk River High student—a sophomore boy—committed suicide. And on the day of that student's funeral, a fifteen-year-old who had dropped out of an Elk River junior high school in the fall also killed herself.

The deaths stunned and numbed district students, parents, and the community. No one was prepared for this.

There were other troubles. Community support for the school district was at a low ebb. The last two attempts to pass a school referendum had been rejected by voters. Facilities were breaking down. There was also dissatisfaction among teachers and talk of a strike.

I believe that Satan specifically targeted Elk River schools that year to make them a stronghold for evil. The enemy had launched an assault.

But I also believe that the Lord knew an attack was coming. It's one of the reasons why He gave me a vision just a couple of weeks before that school year began.

In the vision, I saw two hands bound together with rope. I asked God, "Why are You showing me these hands?"

This is how the teachers feel, that their hands are bound, He said. *I want you to go into the schools and tell them that I know how they feel. Tell the teachers that their hands may seem bound, but their voices are not. Say, "God wants you to begin to call Him back into the schools."*

There was more.

I am doing a new thing, the Lord said. *No longer will you pray on the outside of the schools. Now you will begin to pray on the inside. I want you to take back what has been stolen.*

"Lord, what's been stolen?" I said.

The youth, the land, and the buildings. I want them all back.

I realized that battle lines had just been drawn. I was about to be a solider in a spiritual war. I was ready and willing to fight, but I didn't know how.

"Lord, how do You want me to do this?" I said.

Call the principal of the high school, Jim Voight, and tell him that you want to meet.

I had said hello to Jim Voight before, but we had never had a conversation. I didn't think a high school principal would be open to letting me pray and talk about God with his staff. But Jim agreed to meet with me, and when I asked if I could start a prayer group with teachers after school, he said, "Well, how can I help you?" He also agreed to put an announcement in the school bulletin about the prayer group.

It was beyond what I expected. But then, I have learned that when I am obedient to God, resistance seems to melt away. The doors are always wide open.

Even with this encouragement, I still wanted to be sure that I was hearing God's voice correctly. I asked for a sign. "Lord," I prayed, "if this is truly You, give me at least one teacher who would respond." About a week later, that's exactly what happened—one teacher called, and we met to pray. Soon, however, our prayer group grew to four or five high school teachers at a time.

Our meeting began in October, just a short time after the deaths of the Elk River High junior and the alternative school principal. It was a difficult time at the school. Many students and others were struggling to cope. We had a lot to pray about. I stressed the Lord's message to the teachers: "God knows how you feel. Your hands may be bound, but your voices are not. It's time to call Him back into the schools."

Then I expanded the prayer group meetings into the junior high schools. Teachers there also came together to pray, and we began to see results.

One junior high math teacher told about a student who planned to quit school because his job was too important. We prayed for the student. A week later, the teacher reported that the student had quit his job. He decided that school was more important after all.

On two other occasions, teachers in the district threatened to go on strike. Both times we prayed for unity between the teachers and administration, and both times a strike was avoided.

We were making progress, but the battle was far from over. The two student suicides at the end of January and in early February confirmed that the enemy was still fully engaged.

The Lord gave me further orders: *Go to the school district and tell them that you want to start prayer walking the schools on the inside.* He wanted me to pray for specific sites at the schools and break the stronghold the enemy had there.

I called an official at the school district and explained what I had in mind. Her response was, "The best time to do that is on Wednesday night. No one is there except for janitors."

Again, no resistance. I was even being advised on when I could pray.

The Lord showed me that I was entering into a new level of spiritual warfare. In war, when territory is recaptured, the victors post a flag to tell the enemy that they have regained control. The stirring World War II memorial in Arlington, Virginia, of U.S. Marines planting a flag on Iwo Jima is a perfect example. It is a powerful symbol that after much struggle and sacrifice, the enemy has been driven away.

We began the prayer walks in April at the high school. I invited only a few friends and pastors, but the word spread. Nearly forty people, including parents and students, showed up in front of the school to do battle with the enemy.

My friend Ken Beaudry and I moved to the school entrance, opened a door, and invited Jesus Christ to come in. We established our "headquarters" in the cafeteria, where we played worship music, prayed as a group, and prepared for our mission. Then we sent teams into the school to pray wherever they felt the Lord leading them.

One team of two students sensed "something" down a back hallway. Kathi joined them, and they felt the Spirit pointing them into a classroom, and then to a sketchbook on a desk. They found it filled with drawings of demons, swastikas, and other dark images.

Throughout the high school, we prayed for the Lord to sever all demonic ties and to banish any spirit of rebellion, addiction, witchcraft, or other evil. We prayed for a spirit of mercy and hope to flow through the school and claimed the site as a stronghold for God. We knew we were on the right track when a student passing by noticed the door open, wandered in, and asked what we were doing. A pastor's wife told him we were praying for the schools. Before they had finished talking, she had led him through a salvation prayer.

It was nearly dark by the time we all got back together and gathered at the front of the school around the flagpole. A student pounded a wooden stake into the ground with a hammer. On one side of the stake, written in black marker, was the statement, "Jesus is Lord of Elk River Senior High." On the other side were the words *EverLasting King's River*. We turned the city's name, Elk River, into an acronym with purpose.

We took turns driving the stake deeper. In the darkness, the final blow created a visible spark. We cheered and applauded the Lord, then joined hands around the flagpole and recited the Lord's Prayer. It was the end of a powerful evening.

We took our prayer walks to the junior high and elementary schools as well, sometimes with as many as fifty people praying for God to break through and reclaim His territory. The tide of the battle was shifting. We were pushing the enemy back.

In September 2000—one year after the first student suicide—I attended a prayer breakfast hosted by the mayor. Nearly one hundred fifty city officials and businesspeople were there. Just before the meeting began, Ed Silvoso of Harvest Evangelism, the keynote speaker, asked me to pray for the schools. I had never prayed in public before. I was nervous.

Lord, what do You want me to say? I thought. *How do You want me to pray?*

Chuck, I want you to pray for the new school referendum, He said. *It has failed the last two years, but I am going to see that it passes this year.*

When my time to pray arrived, I stood and addressed the crowd. "The Lord just told me that He is going to get the school referendum passed this year," I said. "He said the physical condition of our schools represents the spiritual condition. He is going to pass the referendum to restore the physical as a sign to us that He is going to restore the spiritual also."

After the meeting, a district school official approached me. "Thank you so much for praying for the schools," he said, shaking my hand. "That was a real encouragement."

As he walked away, the Lord spoke to me.

A new door has just opened to you.

I left the meeting and reflected on this new message from the Lord. I sensed in my spirit that He wanted me to pray with this school official. "When?" I asked.

Tonight.

I was immediately nervous again. "Lord, can't we wait a month or so? Shouldn't I pray more about this? Why tonight?"

I have things I want done right now.

I really didn't want to do this. I had only just met this official. And as with Jim Voight, I expected resistance. Why would he want to pray with me?

"OK, Lord," I said. "If this is truly You speaking to me, I will call him right now. But one, he has to be there. Two, he has to take my phone call. Three, he needs to be receptive to this. And Lord, I am busy tonight, but I have 8:30 available."

So I called. Of course, the school official was in and took my call.

"Sir, the Lord just spoke to me and told me there is unfinished prayer that needs to take place tonight in the high school," I said. "Can you join me, tonight, in prayer at the school?"

I waited for him to say no.

"Well, Chuck, I have two meetings tonight," he said. "One is at 6:00 and one is at 7:00. But I could be there at 8:30."

Once again, the door was open. "That's perfect," I said. "I'll see you there tonight."

Our church is across the street from the high school, and Ed Silvoso was in town that night doing a radio broadcast from the church. I went there, and he and a group of pastors from Elk River prayed for me. Then I started walking over to keep my appointment with the school official.

"Lord, why do You continue to do this?" I said. "I am not comfortable doing this. But You know I won't say no."

Chuck, I know that you will go, He said.

"I'll go, Lord, but I'm not happy."

The school official and I met at the front of the school. We walked in and sat down at a cafeteria table. Other than a janitor somewhere down the hall, we were alone.

The school official looked at me. "OK, Chuck," he said. "What do you have in mind?"

I didn't know what to say. *Here we go, Lord,* I thought. *You're on.*

Immediately, the words came to me. "Sir, we're two men on a mission. You're after the physical reconditioning of the schools, and I'm after the spiritual reconditioning of the schools."

"Don't get me wrong, Chuck," he said. "We want the spiritual here also."

I was surprised. "Perfect," I said. "Then we need to pray. If you lift up the Lord, He will lift you up."

We joined hands and prepared to pray. But the Lord stopped me.

Chuck, you cannot pray with this man yet, He said. *This man has been cursed. The city has cursed him. The city has cursed his family. The city has cursed the schools. The city has cursed the students. You cannot pray with this man with dirty hands. You represent the city of Elk River. You need to repent on behalf of the city and break the curses that have been spoken against him.*

Once again, I was doing battle with the enemy. But I wasn't concerned. The Lord was leading the fight.

I explained to the official what the Lord had just told me. Then I prayed, breaking the curses on him, his family, the schools, and the students. He offered his forgiveness.

Now you can pray, the Lord said. We prayed for Jesus Christ to enter the schools and make His presence felt. We asked God to banish the enemy and his influence from the school district. We also prayed that the $108 million school referendum that would go before voters in November would pass.

Then I asked him if he wanted to pray.

He said, "I don't pray the way you do, Chuck, but I promise you this: I am going to start praying for you. I will pray that God will continue to use you in this way."

When we finished, he gave me an embrace and said, "Thank you."

In the weeks that followed the prayer with the school official, the status of the schools and the referendum received significant media coverage. The newspapers predicted that the referendum would fail again.

They were wrong. It passed by more than two thousand votes. It was another victory in the battle to take back the schools for God.

By the following school year, the official with whom I had prayed had retired and been replaced by another person. The Lord told me to pray with this person as I had with his predecessor. Once again, the door was open to me. Soon God had me inviting many of the area's leading figures to a prayer meeting at Elk River's Salk Junior High School.

As before, I was apprehensive. These were the most influential people in our area. I only knew some of them. Not all were believers. Would they really be willing to invest their valuable time in a meeting dedicated to prayer?

I made the calls; not one person turned me down. We had the mayors of Elk River and Zimmerman, the Elk River School Board chairman, a member of the Elk River City Council, the Elk River chief of police, and the sheriff of Sherburne County, as well as school principals, area pastors, and youth pastors.

Just a year before, it was one school official and I praying for the schools. Now we had a crowd of more than one hundred petitioning God on behalf of the students, teachers, and staff. This time we had two hours of prayer and testimony. At the end of the evening we prayed for the superintendent and the school board. The

Lord told me to repent on behalf of the city and parents for relying on the schools to raise our children. Then the city representatives at the meeting also repented to the district school superintendent and other school officials.

In two short years, so much had changed in the Elk River School District. Relations between the teachers and administration had improved. Though there had been one more student suicide, the rash of student deaths had ended. Most encouraging of all was the change in the spiritual atmosphere in the district. A community had banded together in prayer and lifted the spirit of darkness. The black storm cloud was gone.

I knew there would be more battles against the enemy in the future. But I trusted my Commander. As long as He was in charge, the outcome could only be victory.

Scripture tells us that the devil "prowls around like a roaring lion looking for someone to devour" (1 Pet. 5:8). Against such an enemy, we must be ready to do battle with every available weapon. But our weapons are not guns and bombs. As the apostle Paul said, "The weapons we fight with are not the weapons of the world. On the contrary, they have divine power to demolish strongholds" (2 Cor. 10:4).

The first line of attack or defense in your spiritual arsenal should be the power of prayer. It takes a personal relationship with Jesus based on an active prayer life to resist the destructive influence of darkness. The Bible says we are to "pray continually" (1 Thess. 5:17). Prayer is our connection to the Lord. When we are praying and talking with Him, He makes His power and protection available to us. When the fight is spiritual, it is the only way to win.

Chapter Nine

No Door Will Be Locked

Principle #9: When God opens a door,
your job is to walk through it.

J esse Ventura, the professional wrestler who became a politician, was not considered a friend of the Christian faith by very many people. In one magazine interview he said, "Organized religion is a sham and a crutch for weak-minded people who need strength in numbers. It tells people to go out and stick their noses in other people's business."[1] So I wasn't too excited when he upset other contenders and was elected governor of Minnesota in 1998. I feared that dark days were ahead for our state.

I soon discovered, however, that God's intentions will not be held back. He wasn't about to abandon Minnesota, its government, or its people.

After his victory at the polls, the governor-elect announced that he was going to tour the state and lay out his plan for Minnesota's future. His first stop was to be right in our community, at Elk River Senior High School.

I had no intention of attending. But the day before the event, while praying in my office, I heard from the Lord: *Chuck, it's not a coincidence that Jesse Ventura has chosen Elk River as the first city where he will reveal his plans. I want you to go there tomorrow. I have something I want you to do. I will tell you what it is when you get there.*

I groaned a little when I heard that. I hated not knowing what the Lord was up to. But I did want Him to use me. "OK, Lord," I said. "I'll go."

I felt in my spirit that I wasn't supposed to be there alone. I called the newly elected mayor of Elk River and told her what God had said. Then that evening, after again hearing from God, I called Paul Salfrank, my pastor. "Paul, the Lord has told me that it's our role to bless the state of Minnesota from Elk River," I said. "I don't know how, but you're going to be involved in this. Just show up and be ready."

The three of us met at 6:30 the next morning at the high school. It was a cold morning; I could see puffs of air rising from my mouth as I hurried into the school.

Preparations were underway inside. A huge stage had been erected on the gym floor. I huddled with Paul and the mayor.

"We've got to find the guy in charge here."

A few minutes later, I introduced myself to the Ventura staff member who was coordinating the event. "I work with the pastors in town here," I said. "We would love to officially welcome Governor Ventura to Elk River and bless him. I think it'd be great PR if we could do that."

The staffer seemed receptive. He disappeared for a few minutes, then returned.

"That's a great idea," he said.

We worked out the details. Paul would sit on the stage with the other dignitaries from the governor's office and the Elk River and county representatives. Paul's moment would come after all the other speakers were finished, just before the governor was to be introduced.

Thank You, Lord, I prayed. *We've gone from not even being on the agenda to the best slot on the program.*

Jesse Ventura is a big man, six feet four inches and more than two hundred pounds. He has a mustache and shaved head. Paul, on the other hand, is like a miniature version of Jesse Ventura. He's not much more than five feet tall, has a goatee, and also shaves his head. But Paul speaks from the authority of Scripture, and his words carried the power of heaven that morning.

"We, the church and the city of Elk River, would like to welcome and bless our new governor," Paul said into a microphone when his turn came to speak. The eyes of all the government and other public officials, as well as those of townspeople, the media, and about fifteen hundred high school students, were on him. "I also want to bless the state of Minnesota."

Paul asked Jesse Ventura to come forward, but it wasn't yet time for his formal introduction. "Go ahead, pastor," the governor-elect said. "You can bless me from there."

Though we were in a public setting where prayer was officially banned, the state's new leader had just given Paul permission to pray.

"Please bow your heads," Paul said. He went on to bless the governor, his plans, his staff, other elected officials, and the entire state of Minnesota. At the dawn of a change in leadership, God's Word had been heeded and His sovereignty proclaimed.

When Paul finished, the gym was filled with loud shouts of "Amen!"

The Lord wasn't done intervening for the state. A couple of years later, He told me to go to the state capitol building in St. Paul and begin praying for the government and leaders there. *I want you to do the same thing there that you have been doing in Elk River,* He said. *I want you to pray at the capitol, not outside, but inside.*

Once again, I was uncomfortable. I was being stretched. I didn't even know anyone at the capitol.

I explained the situation to my friend Rick Heeren of the Harvest Evangelism ministry. Rick suggested I call Lonnie Titus, chaplain to the Minnesota House of Representatives. We had lunch, and I asked Lonnie for permission to do prayer walks inside the capitol.

"No one's ever asked that before," he said. "Let me find out."

It seems crazy to think that they would let me do this, I thought. *But it's in Your hands now, Lord.*

A couple of weeks later, Lonnie called to say that my request had been approved. We had permission to go into the house of representatives. I made some calls, and on July 10, 2000, more than one hundred pastors, government representatives, and businesspeople joined me in front of the capitol building. Before going inside, we spent time praising and worshiping God.

As we worshiped, the Lord gave me a vision. I saw Jesus standing in the state of Minnesota. I could see the state borders clearly. In the vision, Jesus picked up the city of St. Paul in His left hand and Minneapolis in His right hand. He lifted St. Paul toward heaven, looked up, and said, "Will You give me St. Paul?"

And God said, "Yes!"

Then Jesus lifted up Minneapolis and said, "Will You give me Minneapolis?"

Again, God said, "Yes!"

Still in the vision, I said to Jesus, "Why was St. Paul the first city that You asked for?"

"Because St. Paul was the firstborn," He said. "I give honor to the firstborn of these twin cities." Then He reached down, picked up another city, and raised that city toward heaven. "Father, if You gave Me St. Paul and Minneapolis, will you give Me this third city?"

God said, "Yes, I will give You this third city."

Jesus continued picking up cities and towns throughout the state of Minnesota, asking God for each one. And the Father said yes every time.

Now, Chuck, the Lord said to me, making a play on words, *"you will be in a* state *of revival.*

I was excited about the vision. The Lord was showing me that we were just beginning.

When we were ready to step into the capitol, I sensed a strong demonic presence. I prayed, "Lord, would You please release two of your warring angels to go into the capitol before us?"

Incredibly, I immediately saw two angels before me, each twenty feet tall. One had a sword, and the other had a huge hammer or mallet. They walked inside and caught a demon that looked like a

Pan god from Greek mythology. It was half man and half animal. The angels bound the demon's hands, laid it on a block of granite, and then crushed its skull with the hammer.

As its head was being crushed, the hand of the demon opened up. A gold key fell to the ground.

The Lord said to me, *Now, with this key, no door will be locked to you.*

We stepped inside. In front of me in the foyer were twelve brass lamp stands, each about seven feet high. One of them was an image of the same Pan god I had just seen in the vision from the Lord. It was confirmation that I could trust in the vision.

We moved into the chambers of the house of representatives, where we faced row after row of empty wooden seats. There, the Lord began revealing to me what He wanted done that evening.

My heart grieves because there has been a separation between church and state, He said. *But My heart grieves even more because there has been a separation between church and church.*

Before I had a chance to explain what the Lord had told me, Rick Hereen, representing the church and a representative from the government repented to each other for the separation between church and state. Rick also brought representatives forward from various church denominations and led them into repentance toward each other. Each one asked the others for forgiveness for the separation between church and church.

Rick then led us into repentance for sins committed against other races. The first repentance was to the Jewish people. He asked a rabbi and his wife to come forward, then read a declaration confessing to and repenting for sins against the Jewish people. The rabbi expressed his forgiveness. Next, a couple with Native American ancestors came to the front of the room. Rick knelt in front of them and confessed to and repented for sins committed against Native Americans. Finally, Rick called all of the young people present to come forward. A group of older men and women repented to the young representatives for sins committed by older people against younger people.

All of this happened within a spirit of love and worship at the center of the seat of our state government. I could hardly believe what I was seeing and hearing.

We finished the evening by going back outside and driving a wooden stake into the ground. Recorded on the stake was a passage from the last chapter of the Bible, Revelation 22.

I learned later that our prayers and confessions had made a difference. Lonnie Titus reported that the capitol staff told him the atmosphere had changed. There was a new spirit of cooperation within the walls of the capitol.

By following God's leading, we were able to help reconcile church and state *and* church and church. During this time, He revealed an important truth: *Chuck, if you listen to Me, I will give you the right thing at the right place at the right time. I will give you anointing and power. Many of My children go out and do good things, even things I have shown them to do, but they get ahead of Me. They do not listen and wait for the right time.*

It was a few months later that the Lord revealed the timing for the next phase of His plan.

Chuck, now I want you to go into the capitol seven times. I want you to tear down the enemy's strongholds over the state of Minnesota. Later, He gave me yet another message. *Do you remember the key I gave you? It's time to go into new areas of the capitol.*

On a cool evening in March, we began to fulfill the Lord's instructions. We prayed in the state house of representatives and other chambers of the capitol, asking for the enemy to be bound and for God's Word, will, and blessings to reign.

The last of our prayer group's seven visits to the capitol was on September 7, 2001. Ed Silvoso, founder and president of Harvest Evangelism, was with us again that night, along with more than a hundred others. Some brought musical instruments. Others carried flags.

We started the evening by releasing a flock of homing pigeons from the steps of the capitol entrance. Then we walked and prayed in the rotunda, the supreme court, the house of representatives, the senate, and through a tunnel to the state office building. Just before we entered the capitol, the Lord said to me, *Chuck, those two angels that went into the capitol with you the first time are still here.*

It was a comforting thought.

Later, Lonnie reported a number of blessings that seemed to flow from these visits. A new spirit of courage and cooperation took hold among the legislators. A higher than usual number of the Lord's followers ran for office during the following months, and each seemed to reflect the same inner call to proclaim the gospel and legislate God-honoring laws. More than thirty separate groups gathered at the capitol to pray after our visits.

In addition, a few years later, thousands of people gathered at the capitol to participate in a crusade led by the evangelist Luis Palau. Even Jesse Ventura seemed to be affected. After our visits at the capitol, the governor was more open to supporting and signing off on initiatives for faith-based programs.

Did our prayer sessions open the door to all those changes? Only God knows the answer to that question. But He had been opening doors for me for a long time, taking me into places where people were not usually allowed in order to advance His kingdom. It had happened with my family and friends. It had happened with customers at work. He had opened doors for me in our city and school district. And now He was allowing me to participate in His plans for the spiritual transformation of the state of Minnesota.

God knows where all the right doors are. All I have to do is follow His lead and turn the key.

So often, we struggle mightily to try to make the "right" things happen in our lives. We attempt to secure a certain job or business deal, find that perfect romantic relationship, or solve a parenting problem through sheer will. But when we make decisions and take action on our own—without relying on the Lord—we almost always end up frustrated and disappointed.

God knows where all the doors are, and He also holds the keys. If you consistently turn to Him in prayer for guidance and genuinely seek to follow His will for your life, He will lead you to the right doorways. Jesus said, "Ask and it will be given to you; seek and you will find; knock and the door will be opened to you" (Matt. 7:7). It's true that following the Lord's path can lead you to some unexpected destinations. But even so, I believe you will end up in the right place every time.

Chapter Ten

RAGING BULL

Principle #10: God's timing is perfect.
He's never late and never early.

For a moment, I thought I was a dead man.

I was in my office at Marquette Bank, where I was a loan officer. I had just returned from lunch and, as usual, was praying at my desk before starting the afternoon's work. But as I prayed, a disturbing picture filled my mind.

In the distance, I saw a bull. He was huge. He was blue. He was angry.

And he was running straight at me.

In my thoughts, I heard the voice of the Lord: *Chuck, don't do anything. Don't move. You move, you lose. I promise you, this thing that is coming at you will not run you over or destroy you. Don't try to fix it. I am going to remove it before it runs you over. I don't care if you are nose to nose.*

The bull was getting closer. I could see two large, thick, very sharp-looking horns pointed in my direction.

Then the vision cleared.

It had seemed so real. But now I was back at my desk. I touched a pile of papers. Everything was just where I had left it. I looked out the window at our parking lot and, beyond it, a farmer's sun-drenched cornfield. Nothing had changed outside either.

I shook my head. I wasn't entirely sure what this message from the Lord meant, but I was again humbled that He was speaking to me—and grateful that I was still alive.

It was the spring of 2000. I had been working for Marquette Bank in the Elk River area for about five years. My family had grown to the point where we could form a basketball team. All of our kids were still at home: Tanner, age twenty, was working at a cable installation company and saving money to buy a house. Rachel, nineteen, was attending a local Bible school and working at a pharmacy. Paula, eighteen; Amber, fifteen; and Taylor, fourteen, were going to school. They were great kids. I was proud of each one of them.

God had blessed us so much. He even communicated to me ahead of time how large our family would be. Before Rachel was born, He told me that we would have either four or five kids. Then, after we had Amber, He gave me a vision of a hand. The four fingers were clearly visible, but the thumb showed only an outline—it wasn't filled in. I knew that the thumb represented a fifth child for our family. Then the Lord told me that our last baby would be a boy. Kathi and I were thrilled, but not surprised, a year later when our second son, Taylor, was born.

I loved being a husband and a dad, and I loved serving the Lord. Life was good.

Little did I know that life was about to change.

The problem, as it had been years before, was our finances. My earnings were based entirely on commission from the loans I arranged. I made a good income at the bank. But business suddenly dried up. Customers started backing out of deals or didn't show up at all. I wasn't doing anything different, yet for some reason deals weren't happening. My income dropped dramatically.

The weeks stretched into months. I was sure the Lord would provide, but I was also concerned. *Am I doing something wrong, Lord?* I prayed. *Are You trying to tell me something?*

The only answer I received, this time while I was driving home, was another vision of the raging blue bull. Only now he was much closer. And he was still running right at me.

One weekend a pastor and his wife from another small Minnesota town came to a worship night at our church. We invited them over for dessert and enjoyed their company.

After dessert, Kathi pulled me into the kitchen. "You know we need to give them some money," she whispered.

"I know," I said. "But honey, we're so broke. I have a check for a thousand dollars, but it's barely enough to cover our next house payment."

Kathi just looked at me. "So, how much?"

Oh, I hate this, I thought. *I should have asked her first how much to give.* The amount that came to my mind was $500. But that didn't make sense. We couldn't afford it. That check for a thousand dollars was all we had.

"Honey, I'm comfortable giving $250," I said.

"OK," Kathi answered.

Immediately I heard from the Lord. *Chuck, keep your comfort money,* He said. *I want your obedience.*

I winced.

"Kathi," I said, my head down, "the Lord just rebuked me. He told me we should give $500."

"Oh!" Kathi said, clapping her hands together and smiling. "That's exactly what He told me."

I frowned. "I don't know what you're so excited about. We've got bills to pay, and God wants us to give half our money away. It just doesn't make sense."

Kathi kept smiling.

Later that evening we said our good-byes to the pastor and his wife and handed them an envelope. I still wasn't entirely happy about giving away so much of our meager funds. But I was even less happy about being rebuked by the Lord. At least I obeyed in the end.

The next day, the pastor called me. "Chuck, how well do you hear from the Lord?" he said.

"Well, I hope pretty well," I said.

"I want you to know you hear right on. After you gave us that envelope last night, I got in the car and told my wife to hand it to me. Before I opened it, I said, 'There's $500 in this envelope.'"

"How did you know that?"

"Three months ago, the Lord told me to go on a missions trip to Brazil, but to not ask for any money. I'm two weeks away from the trip, and last night I still needed $500. I knew what was going to be in that envelope. You hear right on."

I was so encouraged by the pastor's words. I waited for God to bless us for our obedience. Instead, back at my office, I had yet another vision of the angry bull. He was closer still. Now I could see the tips of those massive white horns. I felt like a matador without a cape. But I still didn't understand what God was trying to tell me.

As the weeks went by, our family's funds steadily dwindled. My work at the bank was going nowhere. Our savings were wiped out. Finally, all that was left was a hundred dollars in our checking account.

That night, at a gathering in a friend's basement, we listened to a pastor from California speak about God. Then my friend took an offering—and just like the poor widow who gave two copper coins, I sensed that God wanted us to give all that we had, too.

Kathi must have sensed the same thing. "Do we give it all?" she whispered to me as the offering plate passed in the row ahead of us. I nodded. She wrote a check for one hundred dollars and dropped it into the plate when it came our way. Then I squeezed Kathi's hand. I wasn't sure how, but somehow we would make it.

As our basement gathering broke up, Kathi's brother Richard walked up to us from where he had been sitting in the back of the room. He pulled something small out of his pocket and placed it in Kathi's hand. He said he was walking earlier and picked up an acorn. Then, during the meeting, he heard the Lord tell him, "Give this acorn to your sister and tell her the word *hope*."

Kathi burst into tears. If we needed anything that night, it was hope.

A few days later, I felt overwhelmed by our struggle to stay afloat financially. I left the office and drove to a secluded spot on the bank of the Mississippi River. Like most guys, I don't cry very often. But on this day, I just wanted to let everything go. I sat in my old, white Sunbird convertible—I had just replaced the transmission—and the tears wouldn't flow. I was interrupted by a familiar voice in my head.

Chuck, I'm not going to let you cry. I'm not going to let you feel sorry for yourself.

"But Lord, I want to feel sorry for myself. I want to cry. Come on!"

No. I'm not going to let you cry one tear.

"Why not?"

Because if I let you feel sorry for yourself, Satan's going to add to it. And then it's going to get worse. And by the way, you don't have time for this. Get back to work.

God had "spanked" me again. I wasn't trusting Him. I was looking for my own solution to our problems and not finding one.

I sat in the car a few more minutes, but no tears came. Frustrated, I finally drove back to work.

A few days later, again while praying in my office, the vision of the raging bull returned. This time was more frightening than ever. The bull and I were nose to nose. I could see every detail on his face—fur glistening with sweat, puffs of air exploding from his nostrils, huge black eyes focused directly on me. I was an inch from disaster.

Now I was starting to pick up on the Lord's message, but I didn't like what He was telling me. *Lord, this is too hard,* I prayed. *How can I stay in one place when I'm about to get trampled?*

Our period of financial struggle continued. Finally, despite God's rebukes and visions, I lost the last of my patience. The Lord, it seemed to me, wasn't doing anything this time. I decided that I needed to take matters into my own hands. I put the vision of the angry blue bull out of my mind and faced the facts as I saw them: I needed to provide for my family, and my work at Marquette Bank wasn't cutting it. It was time to leave and find another job. Not long after, I sat down for a first interview at another bank.

My instincts were only half right. God was ready for me to change course. But the direction I had in mind wasn't part of His itinerary, so He blessed me by taking the helm. My "course correction" began at an Applebee's restaurant.

My daughter Paula had invited me out to dinner. We were just taking our seats when I spotted Duane and Patsy Kropuenske at a table nearby. Duane had been executive vice president—and my boss—six years ago when we both worked at another bank in the area. Duane's wife, Patsy, had also been a vice president at the bank. Now Duane was the president of a mortgage company.

I walked over to say hello, and we talked for a few moments. Then I mentioned my plans to leave Marquette and my interview with another bank.

"No, no, don't go anywhere," Duane said, shaking his head. "Come see me first. I need to talk to you."

That's interesting, I thought. *I wonder what Duane is up to?*

Later that week Duane and I met at a restaurant. He explained his plans.

"Chuck," he said, "I don't want you to come work *for* me. I want you to work *with* me. Help me manage the mortgage company, and then eventually we'll start our own bank. You know a lot about mortgage banking, but you don't know much about running a bank. I want to mentor you in banking."

As I thought about Duane's offer, I heard from the Lord. I wasn't sure about Duane's spiritual situation, but I plunged ahead.

"Duane," I said, "the Lord just spoke to me. He said that if you will mentor me in banking, I will mentor you in Him."

"That's a deal," Duane said.

Though Duane was ready to go, I asked him for a little time to pray about it. God had already rebuked me twice. I wanted to be sure that this new direction was part of His will.

At home that night, I asked God for three signs to confirm that this was the way He wanted me to go. The first sign I asked for was an acceptable salary. The second was simply a sense of peace about Duane's offer. And the third was a supernatural sign, something clearly from the Lord. I figured that if God allowed people such as Samuel and Moses to have "burning bush" experiences in Old Testament times, I should be able to have those, too.

That night, the Lord woke me up. I felt Him saying, *Chuck, hurry. Come outside.* I looked at my clock: 3:00 a.m. Groggy, I pushed blankets aside, careful not to disturb Kathi. Again, I heard God speaking: *Get out of bed. Hurry. Come outside.*

As I stood there in our darkened bedroom, another vision came to me. I saw the Lord sitting by a coffee table. On top of the table was a present wrapped in purple-and-white-striped paper and tied together with gold ribbon. The Lord smiled broadly at me and rubbed His hands together. His expression reminded me of a parent anticipating the joy of watching a child open a birthday present.

I got the message. "Lord, I'm coming," I said.

I made my way to the front door and stepped into a cool October night. The sky was clear, and an almost full moon bathed the front lawn in a swash of sparkling silver. I walked a few paces onto our concrete driveway.

"OK, Lord," I said. "What do You want?"

Don't play that game with me, He said. *You know exactly what I want you to do.*

I had been rebuked again. Standing there in my pajamas in the middle of the night, I realized I *did* know what He wanted me to do.

"I'm sorry, Lord," I said. "Please forgive me. I do know what You want."

It seemed strange at that moment, but I felt it was right for me to ask again and formally receive His approval.

"Lord," I said. "Do You want me to leave Marquette Bank and go to work with Duane so we can eventually start our own bank?"

Ask Me for the sign.

"OK, God," I said. "Would You show me Your light?"

At the instant I finished speaking, I spied a glowing ball of brilliant light, roughly a foot and a half tall and about twenty feet in the air, at the corner of my property. The ball suddenly sped across the yard and passed directly in front of me before flying out of sight.

I was stunned. This was the burning bush experience I had asked for. This was the sign. *Wow,* I thought.

Yes, the Lord said. *Now go.*

Soon I was signing a contract to join Duane's mortgage company. On the day I signed, Kathi and I were flat broke. But Duane not only agreed to pay me a generous salary; he also gave me a signing bonus. Later that month, he also paid me my full salary even though I was gone nearly two weeks on a previously scheduled missions trip.

After many months of struggle, our financial circumstances had changed dramatically. The Lord knew what was going to happen the whole time, of course. But I didn't, and I got tired of waiting. I temporarily gave up my trust in Him. Fortunately, He didn't give up on me.

I was so grateful for what had happened. Still, I had to know the answer to one question.

"Lord, why did I have to go through all this?" I said. "Couldn't You have just told me when it was time to leave Marquette?"

I was done blessing you there, but you were too comfortable, the Lord said. *You would not have left. I had to allow you to be uncomfortable so you would be ready to go when it was time.*

Now it all made sense. I understood the meaning of the raging bull vision and His warning: *You move, you lose.* God had been letting me know that trouble was on its way and that He was going to handle it. For that season, all I had to do was...nothing. Then, when it did become time to move, He was there to point the way.

I can still vividly recall that vision of the bull from the Lord. But it doesn't bother me anymore. I understand more clearly than ever that God is in charge of every living creature on this earth, from the angriest bull to the meekest lamb. He will take care of each one in His way and in His timing.

I am just happy to be part of His flock.

I n our fast-paced, modern world, we are naturally inclined to quickly step in and "fix" whatever problems loom before us. It isn't easy to stand still when one of life's crises threatens to run us over.

Sometimes, though, standing still is exactly what the Lord calls us to do. He has known about our trials before they—and we—were formed. He has the perfect plan for resolving every dilemma. He may remove an obstacle from our path at the last moment. He may direct us to an unexpected solution. Or He may want us to experience the hidden benefit of enduring whatever hardship is heading our way.

Waiting on a response from the Lord in the middle of a crisis takes courage and trust. We must be patient and remember the words of Scripture: "To everything there is a season, a time for every purpose under heaven" (Eccles. 3:1, NKJV). Whether our troubles are at home, at work, or in our spiritual lives, we must take them to the Lord. Whatever and whenever His answer, we can be sure it is the right one, at the right time.

Chapter Eleven

A BOUQUET OF ROSES

*Principle #11: God's glory is meant to be
shared. Pass it on, and watch it grow.*

I met Shelly for the first time in a rented office in Elk River. It was the summer of 2002, a few months before Riverview Community Bank opened its doors. It was an exciting time. Duane Kropuenske had hired Shelly to be our operations officer and to help us gear up for the bank's launch. My daughter Rachel, whom we also hired to help with the bank, introduced us.

Shelly had short blonde hair and wore a blue business suit. What I noticed most, however, was how quiet and soft-spoken she was. She was shy and rarely looked me in the eye.

Though we were all delighted with the potential of our new professional adventure, I didn't realize that Shelly was at a low point personally. She was divorced from her first husband. Her marriage to her new husband, Terry, was not at all what she hoped it would be. Terry drank often, and when he did, he bickered with Shelly and their six children. Her eldest daughter, fourteen-year-old Katie, hooked up with some new and, from Shelly's point of view, worrisome friends. Katie had begun dressing all in black. Of even more concern was her new interest in tarot cards, Wicca, and witchcraft.

Shelly was discouraged and losing hope. She didn't know what to do.

I gradually got to know Shelly when I stopped in at the Elk River office to visit Rachel. Shelly's desk was right next to Rachel's. When I visited and began telling "God stories" to my daughter— as I tend to do—I noticed Shelly looking my way. She was listening to every word.

I found out later what she was thinking during my stories: *Could any of this stuff Chuck is saying really be true? How could anyone, even God, love me that much?*

Soon, Shelly was asking me questions about my stories. Did Jesus really have the power to change our lives? What was spiritual warfare? What was a generational curse? I answered and explained as best I could. I was encouraged to see that my stories had planted seeds of interest.

Shelly decided to put some of the wild ideas she was hearing to a test. A friend had been stricken with cancer. She sat down and prayed to the Lord, asking that He remove the malignancy. To her, it felt strange to be talking to an invisible God. But Shelly had to know.

A few days later, she received a phone call that the cancer was gone. Shelly couldn't believe it.

A couple of weeks later, Rachel bought Shelly a woman's study Bible. Then, after more stories and more questions, we invited her to come to our church.

Shelly accepted and met us there the next Sunday. I was surprised and pleased to see she wasn't alone. Her husband and their kids came, too—even Katie, adorned in thick black eyeliner, black-painted fingernails, and a black shirt and pants. Most of the family didn't want to be there, I found out later. But as Shelly explained, "If I was going, I was making sure they went, too."

The service was a shock to Shelly. She usually went to church only on Easter and Christmas and was used to services where everyone sat still and listened quietly. But at our church, the congregation spent much of their time standing, singing, raising hands, and interrupting the pastor with shouts of "Amen!"

These people are so rude to the pastor, Shelly thought. *What's wrong with them?*

Despite her misgivings, however, Shelly found her heart warmed by being there. Something about it felt right. She and her family came back a second time. On her third visit, in the middle of the service, she began to weep.

"I wasn't sure why I was crying," Shelly said. "I thought maybe God was cleansing me. I'd never sensed anything in my heart from Him before that day. But all of a sudden, I felt His love for me."

Soon after, Shelly talked to me about her concerns about Katie. I explained how dangerous her interest in witchcraft and tarot reading was. I advised her and Terry to do a prayer walk in their home, going room to room and, in the name of Jesus, commanding Satan to leave at once. I could see she thought the idea was a little crazy. She had never heard of anything like that.

Soon after, though, Shelly and Terry did do the prayer walk. And Shelly started noticing changes, not only in Katie but also in herself and in her husband. I recommended that Katie check out our church youth group, so Shelly insisted that her daughter go. Katie resisted at first and wouldn't talk to the other kids, but gradually she began opening up and making new friends. Meanwhile, at home, Terry drank and argued less. Shelly felt her anger with Terry start to melt away. She also found herself waking up in the middle of the night with a strange urge to read the Bible.

I saw Shelly at work and asked how things were going with Katie.

"It's gotten better," she said. "I'm really encouraged."

"Good," I said. "I've been praying about that."

"Really? That's a coincidence."

"No, it's not," I said with a smile. "It's a blessing."

A few weeks later, Shelly and Terry were talking with Kathi and me after another service at our church. Shelly asked another question about the Lord. I could see in her eyes how excited she was about getting to know Him.

"Shelly," I said, "if you really want to go further in seeking God, the most important thing you need to do is invite Christ into your life. Would you be willing to do that?"

Not only did Shelly say yes, but Terry, their twelve-year-old daughter Kaylie, and even Katie also wanted to give their hearts to

Jesus. They all saw and felt the changes in their family. Something was happening that they wanted to be a part of. It offered more hope and love than anything they had experienced before.

Right there at the front of the church, as other members of the congregation mingled, Kathi and I led a new quartet of God's children into His eternal family. A few minutes later, Kathi approached Katie.

"You know what, Katie?" my wife said. "When we started praying, I had a vision of a red rose. It was a really tight rosebud. And as we prayed, I saw it open up and blossom. I think my vision was about you. I believe your whole life is about to blossom."

Katie had her head down while Kathi was speaking. When she looked up, there were tears in her eyes.

About two months later, in the middle of the night, Shelly sat up in bed and opened her eyes wide. She had just had the most vivid dream of her life. In the dream, she stood in the middle of a beautiful country, surrounded by trees and green hills. A tall, crooked tree grew out of one of the hills. Nearby was a small house with a grass roof. And she saw children playing.

Strangest of all, she understood the name of this place to be "Awanda." And she somehow knew she was supposed to go there.

Shelly told Terry about her dream. It didn't make any sense to him. When she told her sister about it, she just asked what Shelly had eaten the night before.

Yet the vision of Awanda kept coming back. Shelly was sure God was speaking to her.

A few weeks later, Shelly and her family were at a service at our church. During the time for announcements, our pastor explained that he and a group of pastors from other churches were making a trip to Rwanda, Africa.

Shelly looked at Terry. He looked at her. Breathless, she whispered to him, "That's where I'm supposed to go."

The pastors made their trip. After they returned, they issued a call for the congregation to sponsor Rwandan children whose families were struggling with poverty and the AIDS epidemic. Shelly sponsored a child named Claudine. The vision, however, kept returning.

When our pastor announced that he would be leading a second trip to Rwanda later that year, Shelly attended the meeting for those interested in going. She felt out of place. Many of the people there were business leaders and teachers. Most had much more experience and money than Shelly. The pastor asked each person in the room to describe what they could offer to the leadership team going to Rwanda. When Shelly's turn came, she stammered, "I don't have anything to offer. I just had a dream about Rwanda, and I think I'm supposed to go."

A week later, Shelly received a letter from the church. She was denied a spot on the Rwanda team.

Discouraged, she came to me.

"Chuck, I don't understand this," she said. "I was sure my dream was from God."

"You know what? It was," I said. "But the Lord does everything in His own time. If He wants you to go, the doors will be opened."

Two months before the trip, Shelly received a phone call from the church. Some of the people scheduled to go to Rwanda had backed out. Would she still like to go?

Shelly didn't think twice—she said yes.

But now she had another problem: she had no money to pay for the trip. Everyone else on the team had been raising funds for weeks, but there was little time left for Shelly to do anything. "Lord," she prayed, "can You help?"

A week or so later, Terry received a call from a man they had never heard of, an attorney. Terry's grandfather had died twelve years before, but the attorney had just discovered additional funds from his estate. He would be sending a check shortly.

"Shelly, I think this money is for your trip to Rwanda," Terry said.

Shelly still needed another $401 to cover trip expenses during the two days before they arrived in Rwanda. She didn't know what to do. Then, at a Christian study group meeting, a woman named Lisa walked up to Shelly and handed her a piece of paper. "I think I'm supposed to give this to you," Lisa said. She explained that she had set aside some money for tsunami relief, but for some reason she had never sent it in. Then that day she'd felt a strange urge to give the money to Shelly.

Shelly had never said anything to anyone in the study group about needing funds for the Rwanda trip. She looked down at the paper in her hand.

It was a check for $400.

Shelly started crying and gave Lisa a long hug. She figured she could come up with the last dollar. God had done the rest. He was opening doors faster than Shelly could walk through them.

On October 25, 2005, Shelly departed for Rwanda. There she met Claudine, the eight-year-old Rwandan girl she had been sponsoring the last two years. Claudine recognized her immediately and jumped into her arms. It was a heartwarming "reunion" for both of them. It also inspired Shelly to do all she could to rally support from the citizens of Elk River for the children of Rwanda.

The impact of Shelly's growing faith has spread across continents. It has also spread across generations.

A couple of years ago, Shelly's grandmother Loretta was in a nursing home. She had had a stroke that seriously impaired her ability to speak. Loretta had grown up in a musical family and loved the polka. But now she couldn't even stand, let alone dance. Doctors said that she didn't have long to live. Loretta and the family decided that, rather than have a feeding tube inserted, she would prefer to go to a hospice care facility for her final days.

Shelly had always been especially close to her grandmother. She had been able to talk to her about anything. Now, however, at the end of her life, they could barely communicate at all. It was heartbreaking for Shelly—and doubly so because she wasn't certain if her grandmother had welcomed Jesus into her life.

As the end drew near, Shelly, her mother, and our pastor, Paul Salfrank, all visited Loretta. Shelly had never led anyone to the Lord before. But she did her best one night, telling Loretta about God and heaven.

Loretta seemed to accept what Shelly was saying, but she couldn't form the words to respond. Shelly wanted to be sure. She brought Pastor Paul with her the next evening. Paul read to Loretta and prayed with her. Then he leaned in close and said, "Loretta, do you believe in Jesus?"

Loretta nodded and was able to utter a single word: "Yes."

On the following night, Shelly visited again. Right away, she noticed a peace about her grandmother. There was no fear of death in her eyes. She was ready to meet Jesus.

Shelly crawled into the bed and gently cuddled up next to her grandmother. Words were no longer needed. The love between them was more than enough.

After a period of time—Shelly wasn't sure how long—she carefully pulled away. But Loretta shook her head "no."

Shelly lay back down. "Grandma, I'll come back in the morning," she said.

Again, Loretta shook her head. Then, with great effort, she spoke three words: "I love you." Shelly smiled and wiped tears from her eyes.

The next day, at age seventy-five, Loretta passed away. Shelly consoled her grief-stricken mother. She smiled, gave her a hug, and said, "Mom, now Grandma's doing the polka with Jesus."

Today, Shelly barely resembles the shy, soft-spoken woman I met nearly five years ago. She is growing bolder in her faith every day. She has led a woman's Bible study at the bank and often prays with customers and employees.

It has been a blessing for me these last few years to watch God transform Shelly, Terry, and her family. Shelly is more excited than ever to go deeper in her relationship with Jesus. Terry has stepped up in amazing ways as a spiritual leader of his family. And Katie is a new person. Only recently, she returned from a missions trip to Mexico. As far as I am concerned, they are all a bouquet of roses, blossoming in their new lives with the Lord. I am just grateful to be allowed to sprinkle a little water now and then.

Jesus told a parable to His disciples about a man who sowed seed in his field. The good seed represented sons of the kingdom of heaven. (See Matthew 13:38.) I believe the Lord wants us to sow good seed, too. We should be planting the message of the gospel in as many fields as possible. When we do, we can experience the blessing of watching a tiny seed sprout into a beautiful flower. Better still, we may eventually see that flower produce even more seeds.

Like a pebble dropped on a calm lake that sends ripples in every direction, a single encouraging word, one godly truth, or a lone kind act in the name of Jesus can reach lives we never imagined. When God is involved, even the simplest gesture—such as the telling of a story—can make an impact that lasts for eternity.

Chapter Twelve

JESUS CHRIST, CEO

Principle #12: When you obey God,
He takes care of the bottom line.

Duane Kropuenske and I don't look much alike. He's more than six feet tall, while I top out at five-foot-seven. Our backgrounds aren't too similar, either. Duane attended Augustana College in Sioux Falls, South Dakota, and was raised in the Lutheran church. I ended my formal education after high school and never set foot in a church while growing up.

But Duane and I have at least one thing in common: we both want to be obedient to the Lord. That was clear to me from the moment we sat down in a restaurant and started talking about what the new bank we planned to begin together would look like.

"We don't want this to be just any bank," I said over a hamburger. "We need to invite Jesus to be our CEO."

"Chuck, we can do that," Duane said. "I had a vision twenty years ago that I should build a bank based on strong Christian principles, a true community bank. So that's a great idea."

Since the Lord had told me to join in this venture with Duane, I knew He had plans for the bank and for us. I wanted to commit myself to obeying Him no matter what. I'd given every other part of my life to God. I wanted Him to have authority over my professional life as well.

About a year and a half after our restaurant meeting, in 2002, Duane, Patsy, and I formally began the process of establishing what would become Riverview Community Bank. We created a business plan and dove in.

The first and biggest hurdles we faced were attracting the right investors for our team and raising $5.5 million in capital. I was confident that between us, Duane and I knew enough people who would be a good fit and had the resources to commit to our venture. But after three weeks of calls and visits, we had fewer than twenty investors and less than $2 million in funds. Some of the people who turned us down clearly felt we were out of our league, and maybe out of our minds. They didn't say that, exactly. But I could read it in their faces.

Sometimes I wondered if they were right. My wife and five children, not to mention Duane, were depending on me to make good financial decisions. The Ripkas had just pulled out of a time of hardship. Were we headed right back into more financial trials? It didn't make sense to me that, if God was behind this new bank, we would have so much trouble right from the beginning. More than once I cried out, "Lord, what's going on here?"

Then a prominent businessman in our region decided he wanted to commit $250,000 to our enterprise. Now I was excited—we were turning the corner. But as soon as Duane and I said yes to his proposal, the Lord whispered two words to me: *tainted money.*

I had never heard that phrase before, but I was pretty sure I knew what it meant. *Lord,* I prayed, *why didn't You speak to me sooner? I think You don't want his money. But I can't go to him now and say we've changed our minds. It would insult him.*

We needed those funds badly. I didn't see how we were going to make our target without him. But then I remembered my pledge to obey God—no matter what.

After a few more minutes of reflection, I sensed an answer. I wasn't sure I liked it, but it seemed like the choice God wanted me to make. *Lord, I don't feel released to tell him we don't want his money. Instead, I will pray that You will cause something to happen so he'll find what he feels is a better investment and will withdraw his money.*

I prayed. Then I waited.

Three days later, I was still waiting. Duane and I were discouraged and desperate. We were nearing the end of our list of potential stockholders and didn't even have half of the funding commitments we needed. It seemed the only investors we were attracting were ones the Lord didn't approve of.

I was driving home that night after yet another rejection. I was confused. I had been certain this bank, as well as this partnership with Duane, was the direction God wanted me to go. But now I wasn't as sure.

My eyes were on the road, but my thoughts were elsewhere. "Lord," I prayed aloud, "this isn't our bank. This is Your bank. You need to raise the money. Lord, I want to be in agreement with You. If You want this bank to succeed, I ask that all of your angels go out and begin to whisper in the ears of men and women. I ask that these men and women hear that whisper and come and ask us to be a part of this bank."

I didn't know what would happen, but I felt better after praying. I knew the Lord had heard me and that He wouldn't abandon me. I would just have to wait a little longer to see what His plan was.

I found out about two weeks later. One of the "tainted money" investors was on the phone. He apologized, saying he hoped we wouldn't be offended, but he and his partner had come across another attractive opportunity and had decided to invest their money there instead.

I sighed with relief. *Thank You, God.*

Fifteen minutes later, a familiar face appeared in my office. It was Lloyd, a local building contractor I had known for years.

"Chuck," he said after we exchanged greetings, "I've heard about the bank deal that you and Duane are putting together. I'd like to be a part of it. I want to invest $250,000."

I was floored. Duane and I hadn't even considered talking to Lloyd. Now he wanted to give us $250,000—the same amount our "tainted money" investors had just withdrawn.

Thank You, Lord, I prayed again. *You are a gracious God!*

Not long after, another Minneapolis-area businessperson came to me and said, "Chuck, I'd like to be a $250,000 investor in your bank."

"Great!" I said.

The next day, the man called on the phone. "Chuck," he said, "last night I had a dream, and the Lord said to me, 'I don't want you to be a $250,000 investor in the bank. I want you to be a $500,000 investor.' So I need to invest $500,000."

Over the following weeks, more and more calls came in from people we had never met or even heard of. Some were local, some were from elsewhere in Minnesota, and some were from across the country. They all heard about the bank that was being founded on Christian principles and wanted to invest with us. God was confirming that we were still working within His plan.

There were other signs that we were on track. Twice more, after investors made a verbal commitment to us, I heard the phrase *tainted money* from the Lord. Both times the would-be investors changed their minds and withdrew their funds.

There was the time that Duane and I visited another potential stockholder named Jeff. On the drive to Jeff's office, I hoped and prayed that he would invest a half-million dollars. Then, during the meeting, I also sensed the Lord telling me that Jeff would invest that amount.

At the end of our meeting, however, Jeff said he wanted to invest $60,000 with us—just little more than a tenth of what I had hoped for.

I didn't know where Jeff was spiritually, but I decided to speak up anyway. "You know what, Jeff?" I said. "This may sound strange to you, but I believe God has told me that instead of investing $60,000, you are supposed to invest much more than that."

He sighed. "I would do that," he said, "but I don't have the money now. I have several acres of land that have been for sale for close to a year. If that land sold, then I would be a much larger investor."

By now I was growing more confident in what the Lord could do. "Jeff, tell you what," I said. "Let's see if this is the Lord or not. I'll go to this land site with you and pray for it to be sold. If this is

God, it will sell, and you'll become the investor God wants you to be. How does that sound?"

Jeff agreed to my idea.

"When do you want to go?" I asked.

"Now," he said.

We were gone for three hours. We never even got out of the car. We just drove up to the land and prayed for the buyer to come forward according to the Lord's plan.

Within a few months, the land sold, and Jeff increased his investment.

Over the next several weeks, we moved steadily toward the $5.5 million figure we needed to launch our dream. We were nearly there when I heard from Chris, a chiropractor from Minneapolis.

About three months before, Chris had been driving north on Highway 101 when he sensed the Lord telling him to pull over. He stopped in front of our bank site. Construction on the building had already begun, but there were no signs or billboards indicating just what kind of business was moving in.

Pray for this building and the people who will be in it, the Lord told him. *You're going to be involved with it someday.*

Chris thought that was a little strange, but he was obedient. He prayed over the land and for blessings on the men and women who would eventually be working there.

Weeks later, Chris was talking to a friend in Minneapolis. "I have about $50,000 I'd like to invest," Chris said. "Where do you think I should invest my money?"

"I'm going to invest in this bank in Elk River," the friend said.

"Where in Elk River?"

"Well, it's just off Highway 101."

"I know just what building you're talking about," Chris said. "I've been praying for that place for three months!"

Chris became one of our final stockholders.

At last, thanks to the Lord's blessing, we made it. We had the capital we needed to establish and begin building Riverview Community Bank. God had honored our faith and efforts.

We hosted a traditional groundbreaking ceremony on the site when construction began. But Duane and I wanted to do something more. We wanted to dedicate our dream to Jesus.

It was below freezing on the November day that Duane, myself, and a handful of others gathered in the still unpaved parking lot in Otsego for our little ceremony. A dusting of snow covered the ground. Behind us, most of the frame for our new office home was in place. For a moment, I watched the workers hammer nails into the foundation. It wasn't so long ago that I was pounding nails on construction sites myself, though I'd never felt comfortable doing it. I was grateful now to be called to something I had real passion for.

We gathered around Duane. One of our stockholders handed him a bottle of anointing oil for the occasion. I expected Duane to tip out a few drops onto the frozen dirt, but instead he dumped the entire bottle.

"Lord," Duane said, a little white cloud forming with each breath. "I invite You to be CEO of this bank. I may be the CEO in the natural, but You are the CEO in the spirit. I ask You to guide and direct us in all that we do here, and I dedicate this land, this building, and this business to Your purposes."

Riverview Community Bank opened on March 17, 2003. Engraved on the cornerstone were the words "In God We Trust." That same day, while I prayed in my office, the Lord spoke to me. *Chuck,* He said, *I promise that if you do the things I've called you to do here, I will take care of the bottom line.*

Actually, He had been taking care of the bottom line all along. I just hadn't always had the wisdom to see it.

As if He was eager to erase all doubt, God began giving me visions of numbers. He told me that Riverview deposits and assets would grow to between $25 and $30 million very quickly, that we would reach $42 million in deposits and assets by the end of the calendar year, that we would achieve $52 million within our first twelve months, and that within thirty months, we would possess deposits and assets in excess of $100 million.

I told Duane what God had said and asked what it meant to him.

"Well, that's all impossible," he said. "You don't know it, but I sat down with the FDIC and set a goal for the first twelve months of $16 million. And that's pretty aggressive. We can't grow faster than that anyway. We don't have enough staff."

"Duane," I said, "I believe we're going to meet those numbers *and* that God will bring us the staff we need to do it."

We soon had our answer. By August, we had already hit $30 million in deposits and assets. It wasn't because of our promotional efforts, which were minimal. It just seemed that once the word got out, people were attracted to what we were doing. I had more than one person tell me they felt drawn to the bank, and that once they read the words on the cornerstone, they were ready to make a deposit.

That summer, Duane and I met with a fortyish woman in a matching gray blazer and skirt. She told us she wanted to deposit $1.5 million into our bank. I couldn't help asking why.

"I read a newspaper article about you and your bank," she said. "I'm a Christian. So this is where I want to put my money."

The money kept coming. By the end of December, we had reached $43 million in deposits and assets. After our first full year, we stood at $52 million, just as the Lord had said. And we surpassed $100 million in just twenty-seven months—three months early!

During this same period, employees at a large bank in the area began calling us and asking if we had openings. They saw what was happening and wanted to be part of it. We were able to add experienced employees to our staff just as we needed them.

I wasn't surprised. God was taking care of the bottom line—for my family and me, and for Duane and our entire team at the bank. We had dedicated our dream to Him, persevered during its uncertain beginnings, and now were discovering the amazing plan He'd had in mind from the start.

Despite our dissimilar backgrounds, Duane and I were good partners. But with Jesus as our CEO, we had a team that couldn't be beat.

As a banker and mortgage loan officer, I've closed hundreds of deals over the years. I always think of them as win-win situations—I provide a service to the customer, and the bank also benefits from the transaction. But I have never run across a better deal than the one God offered me the day our bank opened: *Obey Me, and I will take care of the bottom line.*

I can't guarantee that your obedience to the Lord will lead to blessings in this life. Even those who are most faithful to God still experience hardships. But I can promise that your obedience pleases Him and will be rewarded in heaven: "For the Son of Man is going to come in his Father's glory with his angels, and then he will reward each person according to what he has done" (Matt. 16:27).

God is on your side. Through your obedience to Him, the Lord is giving you the opportunity to reap rewards for eternity. If that's not taking care of the bottom line, I don't know what is.

Chapter Thirteen

NEVER SAY NEVER

Principle #13: Your business is your ministry.

I am a businessman, not a pastor. I love to serve the Lord, but I have never felt called to the ministry or to lead a church. I never went to seminary; I don't know the Word well enough. And I can't see myself in front of a congregation preaching a sermon. That just isn't me.

In fact, I used to be so glad I wasn't a pastor that I sometimes praised God for His wisdom in not sending me into the ministry. "Thank You, Lord, for where You have placed me," I would say. "I would never want to be a pastor."

I have learned something since—never say "never" to God.

I discovered my mistake in March 2003, about a week before the grand opening of Riverview Community Bank. Everyone was working hard to prepare for our first day, yet the atmosphere was calm. It appeared we had everything in hand. I was praying alone in my office, asking for the Lord's blessing on our new venture. Suddenly I heard His voice: *Chuck, I want you to pastor the bank.*

I was surprised. "Pastor the bank?" I said. "How do I pastor the bank?"

Take what I have taught you and pass it on to others. Teach others within the bank to pray for the customers. Not only will your customers make physical deposits into your bank, but also you will make spiritual deposits into your customers.

Oh, boy, I thought. *Here we go again.* I had never heard of anyone pastoring a bank, or any other business. But if this was what the Lord wanted, I knew I had better listen.

I had the opportunity to make a spiritual deposit sooner than I expected—and not with a customer, but with Patsy Kropuenske, Duane's wife and the bank compliance officer. It was Sunday, the day before the bank was to open. I was having brunch with my wife, Kathi, at a restaurant near the bank when Duane and Patsy walked in. I went to greet them and saw Patsy gritting her teeth.

"Patsy, what's wrong?" I asked.

"I'm in terrible pain," she said with a grimace. "I can barely walk." Patsy's whole body ached. She had seen a chiropractor the day before who said her muscles were so tense there was nothing he could do.

"Patsy," I said, "the Lord just showed me something for you. You don't have a physical problem. You have a spiritual problem." I had never spoken to Patsy this way before, but I knew I was supposed to share what I had been told. "The Lord showed me you've been cursed all your life. Those curses have stuck to you, you've believed in those curses, and they're causing you physical problems. You're like a pincushion.

"The Lord told me how to get rid of these curses. I don't know why, but He wants us to do it over at the bank."

Patsy was so uncomfortable that she was ready to try just about anything. Soon we had all gathered around her in a large office at the bank. My daughter Rachel, who was working at the bank, joined us. Kathi led Patsy in a prayer of repentance for receiving and believing in the curses. Patsy renounced the curses. Rachel prayed for Patsy. Then I prayed to break the curses that afflicted her. As I prayed, Patsy felt a surge of heat in her hands.

When I was done, she looked at me intently. I thought I saw a glimmer of hope in her eyes.

Again, the Lord spoke to me.

"Patsy," I said, "you are going to be 100 percent healed in the next twenty-four hours."

I don't know if she believed me. But to Patsy's great relief, she woke up in the morning with no aches or pains. When she saw her chiropractor later that day, he was amazed. "You're in perfect shape," he said. "Before, there was nothing I could do. Now there's nothing for me *to* do."

Our time with Patsy the day before the bank opened was the first healing ever performed at the bank. But it wouldn't be the last. On Tuesday of that week, a customer came by to visit Patsy at her office. She had a severe limp from a past injury. A doctor had told her that she would have this limp for a long time. When I was introduced to her, I sensed that I was supposed to intervene.

"Could I pray for you real quick?" I asked. She agreed. I knelt down and briefly asked the Lord to heal this woman's leg.

At the end of the week, Patsy was scheduled to meet with this customer again. Patsy was surprised to see the customer walk into her office without a limp. She was completely healed.

About four months later, an elderly woman from Minneapolis called me at my office. "Is this the bank that prays for people?" she asked. The stories of the healings had spread. Soon we were getting calls from other people who wanted to come to the bank and have someone pray for them and their troubles. Every couple of weeks, someone would come to my office to ask specifically for healing prayer. Even more amazing, God seemed to heal most of them almost immediately.

One day, I received a call from a pastor I had never met. He heard about me and wondered if I would be willing to pray for someone. A man now in his thirties had accidentally been dropped on his head as a two-year-old. The fall left him with crushed vertebrae and pain that still plagued him after thirty years. Soon this man was in my office—and so was the pastor. The pastor had been suffering from back pain, too. I prayed for both, and both told me within moments that their pain was gone.

Yet my duties as "pastor" of the bank included more than praying for others. The Lord also wanted me to encourage our staff to pray. He showed me that I should start with Gloria Oshima, a teller and a strong believer.

During our opening week, I said to Gloria, "The Lord has told me that you're going to start praying with customers at the drive-through."

"Really? Me?" Gloria's eyes were wide. I could see she was excited about the idea.

About six months later, a young lady pulled up to the drive-through window during Gloria's shift. The woman had tears in her eyes.

"Are you OK?" Gloria asked. "Would you mind if I prayed for you?"

The woman said OK.

"Inside the bank or right here?" Gloria asked.

"This is fine here," the woman said.

Gloria prayed for the Lord to remove the woman's hurts and bless her day. Later, the woman returned to the bank lobby to speak to Gloria. "I'm doing so good," she said. "I just wanted to thank you for your prayers."

Since that day, Gloria has prayed for and blessed many customers. She has the gift of mercy and can usually sense when someone needs prayer. None of the customers have ever turned Gloria down when she asks if they need prayer.

Gloria isn't alone in her ministry. During the first three years since Riverview opened its doors, I prayed with nearly every member of the staff, almost sixty people. Twenty-one of them invited Christ into their lives. And many, just like Shelly Nemerov and Gloria, began praying with customers when asked or when they felt God's Spirit moving them.

As I watched and participated in everything that was happening, I couldn't help shaking my head at what God was doing. I was praying with two or three customers or employees a day. One day I prayed with thirteen people! I spent so much time talking with the Lord on behalf of others that I had to work into the evening to get my bank business finished.

It was an amazing time. I was hearing from God more often than ever, and His answers to prayer requests seemed to be coming faster and faster. Something phenomenal was happening.

I realized just how much had changed on a summer day in 2004. I was walking out the door of the bank for a meeting in Elk River when a man in a tracksuit and his pregnant wife asked to see me. They were struggling. He was in ministry, and his church was in financial distress. They were about to have their fifth child. They needed $80,000 as soon as possible.

But this couple wasn't coming to me for a loan. They needed spiritual encouragement. The woman said the Lord had told her to come and pray with me.

So I prayed with them in the parking lot. I asked Jesus to give them peace, strength, and guidance. Then I asked them to join me at my meeting. It was a gathering of our Pray! Elk River team. The couple sat on metal chairs in the middle of the room, and twenty-five of us prayed for them, their ministry, and their family. The woman began to cry as we called on God to bless them. Then someone in our group suggested we take an offering for them. They were overwhelmed.

Later, it occurred to me that this couple and I had reversed roles. A man in ministry and his wife had come to a mortgage banker for spiritual guidance and prayer. Maybe, in a way, I was a pastor after all. My church was the bank. My pulpit was my office. My congregation was the customers and employees that I counseled, encouraged, and prayed with every day.

The media described what we were doing as the "faith-at-work movement" and participants as "marketplace Christians." I was familiar with the terms. I was already practicing it in my work and in the community. But since God told me to pastor the bank, I came to understand just how important my work was to Him. He wanted to be at the center of *everything* in my life, including my career. I was seeing what could happen when I fully embraced Him at the office as well as at church and at home.

In God's eyes, my business was my ministry. And this ministry wasn't confined only to Riverview. It was spreading.

I remember a young woman who came into the bank for a loan. Her name was Karen, and before she said a single word, I knew she was upset. There was a heaviness about her. It was as if a shadow loomed over her wherever she went.

By the time we finished going through her application, I was sure I was supposed to pray with her. *Lord, please open the door,* I prayed.

Tell her what you do, He said.

That was easy enough. "Karen," I said, "before you leave, I just want you to know that I usually pray with my customers. If it's all right, I'd like to pray with you."

Karen looked surprised at my request, but she agreed.

"Karen, if you could ask God for anything today, what would it be?"

She said that I could pray for her two children. But then I heard the Lord's voice: *No, that's not it.*

That was unusual. I had never heard those words from the Lord after a prayer request.

I prayed for Karen's children. Then I said, "Karen, is there one more thing that we could pray about today?"

She thought for a moment. Then she said that she'd been struggling with money. We could pray that her financial situation improved.

Again I heard from the Lord. *No, that's not it either.*

I was puzzled. I went ahead and prayed. Then I took a deep breath. I didn't want to be pushy, but clearly the Lord had more for our agenda.

"Karen," I said, "could there be just one more thing that we should pray for?"

Karen stared at me until her eyes began to well up. Then she put her head down. Softly, she began telling me about how a person who had been in prison for sexually abusing one of her children was now about to be released.

"I'm afraid," she whispered. "I don't know what this person's going to do."

This time I didn't hear anything from God. We hit the spot.

I prayed for protection for Karen and her children. I prayed for healing and peace for the person who had abused her child, and for any feelings of anger or bitterness to fall away.

When we were done, Karen smiled broadly and thanked me. I thanked the Lord for urging me to dig deeper into this young woman's prayer needs.

About two weeks later, Karen returned to the office to complete her loan. Her step was lively; she almost glowed when she came in. She didn't seem like the same person.

"Karen, what's going on?" I said. "You look so different...so happy."

"It was those prayers," she said.

"What do you mean?"

"Chuck, everything that we prayed for, God has answered," she said. "I got a raise at my job. I have forgiven the person who hurt my child, and I'm not afraid anymore. I also want you to know that now *I'm* praying for people at my work, just like you. Thank you so much!"

When Karen left, I think I felt even more encouraged than she did. It is such a blessing to see God change lives and to know that He is using me to accomplish that. What could be more rewarding? Sure, I strive to succeed as a banker and businessman. I take pride in my work, and I feel a strong sense of satisfaction when we close a deal or exceed our goals.

Yet none of it compares with doing God's work. Everything I have achieved at Riverview or anywhere else is because of Him. He is the reason I am here.

Pastor the bank? Why not? I know I am on the right career path if I am doing business with the Lord.

On the wall in Duane Kropuenske's office at the bank is a large color print of two men in business suits talking with Christ. They are in an office setting. A laptop computer sits on the desk, and city skyscrapers can be viewed through the window. Jesus is shaking hands with one of the men, almost as if they are closing a deal.

The image is a visual reminder of what we all must remember: the Lord is fully present at the office and very much a part of everything we do at work. If we put up walls to keep God out of our business dealings, we are erecting barriers to a personal relationship with Him and to His plans for us. We can't expect the Lord to bless our work lives if we ignore Him every Monday through Friday.

The print of Jesus, created by an artist named Nathan Greene, is appropriately titled "The Senior Partner." The next time you are weighing a business decision, you might ask yourself: *What would the Boss think?*

Chapter Fourteen

DREAMS

*Principle #14: God may call on you
at any time, for any purpose.*

I had just settled into an easy chair in my basement when the phone rang. It was my friend Jay Bunker. "Chuck, I need to talk to you about a dream I had three weeks ago," he said.

That sounded a little odd, but I knew Jay wouldn't bother me with something trivial. I respected Jay. He was the pastor of a church in Elk River for thirty-five years. More recently, he has been serving as part of an outreach team to inmates in the Sherburne County Jail.

"Sure, Jay," I said. "What was the dream about?"

"Paul Wellstone."

Now I was even more surprised. Paul Wellstone had been a U.S. senator from Minnesota since 1991. He was Jewish and known as the most liberal representative in the senate. He had voted in favor of abortion rights, against school prayer, and against funding for sexual abstinence education. Now it was October 2002, and Wellstone was bidding for a third term in office. The election was only a couple of weeks away.

Jay told me about his dream. He saw Paul Wellstone standing in a cemetery. Wellstone was looking at gravestones and contemplating his salvation.

When Jay woke up, he said, "Lord, why did You give me a dream about Paul Wellstone? I don't even care for him."

Call Chuck Ripka, the Lord told Jay. *He'll know what to do.*

Jay found the experience strange; he hesitated about talking to me. But he had finally made the call.

I thanked Jay for letting me know and said I would pray about it. The truth was that I didn't have any idea what Jay's dream meant or what I was supposed to do about it. I had never met Paul Wellstone, and I often disagreed with his political stands and decisions. But I felt the Lord would let me know about the meaning of His message when He was ready.

About a week later, Kathi and I flew to Colorado for a conference. It was Wednesday, October 24. I was tired that evening and fell asleep quickly in our hotel room. But at 3:00 a.m., something woke me up. In the next instant, I realized that it was the Lord.

"Lord, what do You want?" I whispered.

I want you to pray for Paul Wellstone.

"For what?"

Pray for his salvation. Chuck, I know your heart. I know that you do not care for this man. I don't care for all that he stands for. But I still love the man. Pray for his salvation.

I have to admit that I didn't feel much like crawling out of bed that night. Paul Wellstone was not someone I normally would have prayed for. And I was so tired. But I did want to remain obedient to the Lord.

Another thought struck me as I lay there in the dark. A couple of years before, the Lord had told me, *Chuck, I will never waste your time.* I realized that God must have had His reasons for waking me up right then.

"All right, Lord," I said, carefully pulling back the covers. "I'll pray."

For the next thirty minutes, in my pajamas, I sat in a chair in our room and prayed for Paul Wellstone to come to know the Lord. Knowing that he was Jewish, I asked for the love of Jesus to wash over him and for his eyes to be opened to see Christ as his Messiah and Savior. I prayed that his soul would only find rest in Jesus.

Finally, I felt released to end my prayer time. I slipped back into bed and promptly fell asleep.

The next day, Kathi and I were on our way to lunch when we passed a television in the hotel lobby. A news reporter was saying something about Paul Wellstone.

"Kathi, wait a minute," I said. "I want to hear this."

The TV showed a still image of Senator Wellstone. The news was unbelievable. Paul Wellstone, his wife, his daughter, three campaign staff members, and two pilots had been in a plane that had gone down near Eveleth, Minnesota. There were no survivors.

The plane had crashed at approximately 10:22 a.m. central standard time—less than six hours after I had finished praying.

I was stunned. I spent the rest of the day thinking about my prayer and that plane crash. I recalled God's promise to never waste my time. Then I remembered another message from the Lord— that no one would rebuke a word He gave me as long as I acted on it in His timing.

As I weighed these ideas, I came to an important conclusion: Paul Wellstone must have prayed and accepted Jesus Christ into his life before the plane crashed. Why else would the Lord give a vision to a retired pastor and have him tell me about it? Why else would God wake me up in the middle of the night—Paul Wellstone's last night on earth—and have me pray for a man I had never met and with whom I had nothing in common?

I learned later that the plane's airspeed dropped suddenly as it approached Eveleth-Virginia Municipal Airport, just before it plummeted to the ground. Early investigations into the crash speculated that ice on the wings may have contributed to the accident and that the passengers on board may have had several minutes of warning that they were in trouble. The final National Transportation Safety Board report, however, blamed the tragedy on pilot error. It said the pilots waited too long to lower the plane's landing gear, and when they did finally lower the gear, the plane slowed and stalled, crashing just a quarter-mile from the runway.

I don't know for sure what happened on that plane. But I did discover that Sheila Wellstone, Paul's wife, was raised in a Christian home. She must have known the truth about Jesus. And others told me that Paul Wellstone had been in many Christian settings and worship services over the years. He would have heard the gospel message a number of times.

I believe that the Lord was working in Paul Wellstone's spirit during the last weeks of his life. And in those final, frightening moments—when he knew it was now or never—I believe he committed himself to Christ.

In some ways, it seems strange that the Lord would choose two Christians with no connection to or any interest in a liberal Jewish politician to be the means to his salvation. But we have a big God with a big heart. His words "I still love the man" are a not-so-subtle reminder that He desires to bring every one of His children into His kingdom, that He grieves when even one is lost, and that He will use any of us to accomplish His will.

The more I thought about it, the more I was glad that God had trusted me with praying that night for Paul Wellstone. I hope that I was right—that Paul was now rejoicing in heaven with our Lord. I look forward to meeting him and sharing about what happened.

Though none of us deserve His love, God cares deeply for each one of us. And for that, I am eternally grateful.

As a parent of five children, I think I have at least some understanding of God's attitude toward all of us, His children. He desires our obedience. He also, out of love, desires to teach us more and more about His ways and what is best for us. And as we learn to obey and walk in step with Him, He is able to trust us with increasing responsibility.

Part of that responsibility is being available to God twenty-four hours a day. There is nothing as rewarding as working for the kingdom, but it is not a part-time position. We are never "on vacation" from God. When He trusts us, He will use us whenever and however He sees fit.

I certainly wasn't expecting to hear from the Lord during that the early morning I prayed for Paul Wellstone. But I'm so glad now that I didn't ignore His voice or postpone my prayer. I feel privileged that He trusted me with such an important mission—the opportunity to win another man's soul. When the Lord calls on you, I pray that you will be ready to trust Him just as He trusts you.

Chapter Fifteen

SECOND CHANCE

Principle #15: Your life is a gift from
God, so give it back to Him.

My scrambled eggs were getting cold, but I made no move to touch them. I was too busy getting to know the young man sitting across from me in the restaurant booth.

Christopher R. Olson had asked to meet with me so we could discuss a loan he wanted to arrange. Chris was about thirty, a slender, soft-spoken man who was the owner of a financial planning company in Elk River. He was enjoying considerable success in his business. But it was his spiritual status that Chris was most interested in talking about. He wanted to go deeper in his faith and take risks for God.

"Chuck, I've been seeking what you have for a long time," he said. "My life is so good. But I'm too comfortable."

Chris told me about some of his frustrations as a businessman. He felt he spent so many hours tending his business that he didn't have time for ministry. I said that one need not be separate from the other, that his business *was* his ministry.

Chris and I got so wrapped up talking about God that morning, we didn't get around to discussing his loan until weeks later.

A few months after that, Chris invited me to speak at his company. He wanted his employees to have the opportunity to hear some of my stories and learn more about God. I gladly accepted his offer, but it occurred to me later that Chris was the one who should offer his testimony. The Lord has given Chris a second chance at life. He is a walking miracle.

The miracle began on a summer day when Chris was eighteen. While looking in a mirror, he noticed a large bump near the top of his head. He didn't remember crashing into anything there, but he was an active guy. He figured it was a bump that would go away, and a couple of weeks later it did disappear.

That fall, however, Chris noticed an indentation in his skull, about the size of a silver dollar, in the same spot. His buddies at the construction site where he worked were freaked out—they could press on the spot and the skin folded in as if nothing was there.

This time, Chris decided he'd better have a doctor take a look. He visited a general practitioner on a Monday. That doctor recommended a specialist. Soon Chris was undergoing CT and bone scans.

On Thursday of that week, Chris met yet another doctor in a building that looked more like an office than a medical facility. The doctor had trouble looking Chris in the eye. He didn't seem to know how to begin.

"I think you should sit down," the doctor finally said.

Uh oh, Chris thought.

The doctor told Chris he had an extremely rare cancer. The cancer had wrapped around his skull, eaten a hole through it, and formed a tumor inside his brain. He led Chris into a room filled with X-rays clipped to the wall. The tumor was huge.

The doctor recommended immediate surgery. He added that he needed to be honest—the tumor was severe. Even if they were able to remove the tumor, there was a significant chance Chris would lose his memory or end up paralyzed. They only found one previous example in medical history of a person with the same kind of tumor in the brain.

The doctor didn't say if that person survived. Chris didn't ask.

Chris went home numb. He thought he had his whole life ahead of him. He had plans to conquer the world. Now his world had just come to a crashing halt. Suddenly, his relationship with God—which was real, but often distant—took on a new urgency.

The doctors wanted to operate the following Monday, but Chris talked them into waiting a week. There were some people he wanted to see.

One of those people was Father Mark Stang. A few years before, while studying to become a priest, Mark was diagnosed with a severe case of intestinal cancer. Because he was in the hospital and Catholic church officials believed he might not live to achieve his ordination, they made an exception to the rules and allowed him to be ordained early. When Father Mark returned to the hospital after his ordination, his doctors were amazed. The cancer was gone. He was completely healed.

Chris and his brother, Kevin, went to the church that Sunday evening to talk to Father Mark. At the same time, a group that included my friend Ken Beaudry was meeting in the church attic for prayer. Soon they all gathered around Chris, placed their hands on his head and shoulders, and petitioned the Lord for blessing and healing.

As they prayed, Chris uttered his own silent plea. *God, I know You can't fix this hole in my head right here, right now.* (Later, Chris realized that wasn't true—God *could* have fixed the hole if that was His will.) *But surely,* Chris prayed, *You can take away this tumor.*

When they finished, Chris felt light as a feather. All the anxiety from the past week was gone. It had been replaced by a supernatural sense of peace.

He knew he had been healed.

Chris and his family left the next day for a vacation in Colorado. Chris told them and some friends that he had been healed at the church. His cancer was gone. The expression on many of their faces seemed to say, "Poor Chris. First cancer, and now he's losing his mind."

Kevin, who wasn't able to join the family on their trip, also felt an assurance that Chris had been healed. When people called to offer their support, Kevin told them not to worry and that the Lord had healed his brother.

The following Monday, Chris and his family arrived for the surgery. His parents and his brothers and sisters were apprehensive.

A doctor told them that if the surgery took several hours, that would be good news. It would mean the doctors believed they could extract the tumor and insert a plastic cap in Chris's skull. But if the surgery took only a few hours, they would need to prepare for the worst. It would mean the tumor had spread too far and that the doctors felt it best to let it be.

Chris, however, was excited that morning. He wanted to tell the neurosurgeon about his healing. He finally got the chance just before the surgery. Chris explained the whole story.

The neurosurgeon smiled. His eyes were patient. "That's great, Chris. I need all the help I can get."

Forty-five minutes later, the neurosurgeon left the operating room and gathered Chris's family in an anteroom. His face was ashen. Chris's parents and siblings were brokenhearted. They understood what this sudden meeting meant. Most had tears in their eyes.

The neurosurgeon looked down and shook his head. "I don't understand it," he said. "All the CT scans and bone scans showed the tumor. And the hole is still there in Chris's skull, but the tumor is completely gone."

Chris's family—except Kevin—couldn't believe what they were hearing. Their downcast looks turned to smiles. It was a miracle.

A few hours later, Chris woke up from the surgery and opened his eyes. He was surrounded by rejoicing family members who were thanking and praising God for Chris's healing.

Chris was happy, but also a little perplexed. *This is odd*, he thought. *I've been telling them I was healed for the last week.*

In the years since, the Lord has used the story of Chris's healing to touch many lives. And Chris himself has developed a more intimate relationship with God as well as a growing desire to fulfill His purposes.

I was a part of those purposes on the day I spoke at Chris's office. My brother-in-law, Richard Sicheneder, along with Chris and twelve associates met around a long table in a conference room. I was nervous. I wasn't sure how Chris's staff would receive my stories. I found out later that Chris was nervous, too, wondering the same thing. He knew that not everyone on his team was a believer, and he hadn't had the chance to tell everyone what I was going to talk about. Yet he felt it was important that they all be there.

I told several of the stories about how God has moved in my life and how obedience has brought me closer to Him and His will. I ended up talking about God for forty-five minutes and what we did at our bank for about thirty seconds.

During my presentation, everyone seemed quiet and focused. But I really couldn't tell what they were thinking. At the end, I offered to stay longer and pray individually with anyone who was interested. Then Richard and I walked from the conference room to a smaller office to see if anyone would show up.

The response was overwhelming. Every man in the room wanted individual prayer. One man, Tedd—the staff member Chris feared would be most resistant to my message—even pushed past another so he could go first. He explained that he had an appointment and needed to pray right away.

Two of the men we prayed with wept openly as we talked. "You're telling me more about God, about how real He is, than I've ever heard before," one said. "You've exposed me to who God really is."

Another confessed that he had been running from God. His wife had had an affair, leaving him devastated. He turned to drugs. Now he was willing to pray for God's help. Two other believers recommitted their lives to the Lord.

I stayed at Chris's office for as long as I could, then Richard finished praying with those who were left. I couldn't believe how many lives were being changed by this one visit.

We soon discovered that the Lord was just getting started.

Richard was already leading a group prayer ministry from his home, but I was encouraging him to expand what he was doing into the marketplace. The meeting at Chris's office seemed a perfect example of what could happen if we took God's Word into the business world. We had a group of "intercessors" for our bank—people who regularly prayed for God's protection, favor, and guidance for the bank and staff. But many more businesses desperately needed intercessors.

Richard was hesitant to take this step, so I decided to nudge him along. I prayed one morning for his automobile auction business to slow down so that he would have more time for ministry. That same morning, I received a call from Chris Olson asking if I or someone else could become an intercessor for his business.

I recommended Richard.

Within a month of our appearance at Chris's office, Richard and other members of his team were leading prayer groups and Bible studies at Professional Resource Group. They prayed for a kingdom vision for the company, that the staff would know God's truth, and that God would bless the business and each employee.

During that first week after the prayer sessions, Chris had meetings with three clients who each had greater investment potential than any of his previous clients. He felt that God was trying to tell him something.

Tedd, the first man Richard and I prayed with at Chris's office, was also receiving a word from God—but it was a very different message.

Richard and others met with Tedd during those first weeks to talk more about God. After the first of those meetings, Tedd noticed that the aspen tree in his office—which had been dying—was now springing back to life. He took it as a sign that God wanted him to continue meeting with the prayer team.

Not long after, it became apparent that Tedd had developed a different philosophy than Chris's for the business. It created friction between them. The situation reached the point where Richard, Chris, and Tedd met to discuss how to handle their differences. They consulted the Book of Matthew and read the Lord's instruction about how brothers should respond to sins against each other. (See Matthew 18:15–17.)

By the end of that meeting, Tedd had decided it was time for him to move on. But instead of lashing out at each other, both men leaned on God's wisdom as they parted ways.

"Chris, I feel that God is telling me to leave the company," Tedd said.

"If you feel that's what God wants you to do, I'm not going to try to stop you," Chris said. "You've got bigger and better things ahead of you, so I release you to do that. I still want to consider you a friend."

"I feel the same way," Tedd said as they shook hands.

Eventually, five of Chris's associates left the firm to pursue other interests. But the turnover led to a more cooperative attitude among the remaining and new members of the team. Even clients seemed more comfortable and at peace. The change was positive.

Unlike Tedd, Bill, the company's chief operating officer, resisted the new spiritual movement at the office at first. He seemed to not want anything to do with Richard or me. I felt I could almost read his thoughts: *What are you guys doing here? What do you really want? I don't trust you.*

Bill was having trouble with his child, however. The day finally arrived when he came to Richard for help. Richard talked to him about spiritual warfare and advised him on doing a prayer walk in his home. Bill was willing to give God a chance. He took the bottle of anointing oil that Richard gave him and went to work. Bill says he used so much oil that "all [his] doors [were] stained."

The prayer walks made a difference. Within a month, Bill reported significant changes in his child's behavior and in their relationship. Now Bill is studying to lead one of the Bible study classes at the office. He tells others, "You need to listen to this stuff. Prayer works!" Other staff members are also going deeper in their spiritual walk. Some are visiting hospital patients and leading them to the Lord.

Clearly, God is working in the marketplace and making a difference in people's lives. As Richard says about his own experience, "It's stretched me big-time. You can hear and walk in faith, but to see it happen is another thing. Now I have firsthand experience. It's been a real faith-builder for me."

The biggest change of all at Professional Resource Group may be within Chris himself. During that first week of meetings, Richard and I anointed Chris as pastor over the office. It was a new role for him. He didn't have much experience praying with others and asked for our guidance. But just a few days later, he was given the opportunity to share his testimony three times in a single day. Now he's much more comfortable praying with associates and clients when he senses the Lord's direction.

Chris has noticed other changes, too. He used to spend hundreds of hours each year making backup plans for financial issues facing the company and his clients. Today he spends less energy on unnecessary contingency plans and more on trusting God to handle problems and emergencies.

It is exciting to see what God is doing for Chris and through Chris. His business is flourishing, and I know Chris gives back generously to the Lord's work. And he is finding other ways to serve through his business.

One example is a weekend conference I recently hosted in Elk River, "Encountering the Father's Love," led by pastor and author Jack Frost. Chris sent a letter to each of his clients, telling them about the conference and offering to pay all their fees if they wanted to attend. Seventy-five clients did exactly that, and many of them let Chris know what a difference it was making in their lives.

I love meeting people like Chris. He is enthusiastic about his faith and about his relationship with the Lord. He was given a second chance at understanding what God's love and grace are all about. Now, because he desires so much to give back to the Lord he loves, many of his associates and clients are also getting that second chance.

At eighteen years of age, Chris Olson was staring
death squarely in the face. The prognosis for
his cancer was far from promising. He knew there
was a very good chance he was about to die.

But Chris also knew whom to turn to in his
desperation. I don't know why God grants miracles for some and not for others. In reality, though,
every day is a gift from Him. When the Lord took
away the tumor in Chris's brain, He gave Chris a
second chance at life. But really, that is what He did
for all of us by dying for our sins on the cross. At
that terrible and wonderful moment, we all gained
a second chance to enter into His marvelous plans
for us, all the way into eternity.

Like Chris, you have a second chance at life. I
urge you to make the most of it!

Chapter Sixteen

INTO NATIONS

*Principle #16: To walk closer with
God, overcome your fear of man.*

I had never been to Argentina. I had never even been out of the country. But after praying about it, Kathi and I decided to join a team that was going to Argentina. Ed Silvoso, founder and president of Harvest Evangelism, was leading the trip.

Kathi still had reservations. We didn't know what to expect in Argentina. We didn't speak Spanish or know much about the culture. She wondered if it was wise to leave our three teenagers at home on their own for ten days. But we both felt the Lord wanted us there, so in October 2000 we found ourselves on a jet plane, descending out of the clouds into Argentina's capital city, Buenos Aires.

The size of the city blew me away—block after block of buildings and homes. Roughly three million people live within the city limits, and another thirteen million live in the surrounding area of Buenos Aires Province. I had never seen so many taxis. We were definitely not in Elk River anymore.

A few days after our arrival, Ed announced that he was taking a small group the next morning to meet the president of Argentina at the "Pink Palace," the stately home of the ruling government.

Several minutes later, I approached Ed. "Ed, the Lord just spoke to me," I said. "I'm supposed to come with you tomorrow."

"Chuck, that's impossible," he said. "We had to send copies of our names and passports and visas months ago for their security people. It would a miracle if you got in."

"Well, Ed, what kind of business are we in?"

He chuckled. "OK," he said. "You can come. But I can't guarantee you'll get in."

As I lay in bed that night, the Lord spoke to me again. He told me to bring the camera I had borrowed, an expensive Canon with a zoom lens, to the meeting. I was to be the group's photographer, He said, and should be introduced that way to the Argentine officials.

When we arrived at the palace the next day, security guards lined us up outside and checked our credentials. I was last in line. Everyone was on the approved list, of course, except me.

The guard looked at me, then at his list with every name checked off.

Lord, is this really going to work? I thought. *I guess we're about to find out.*

The guard pointed to me and said, "Who is he?"

"He's our photographer," someone said.

The guard looked at my camera and the equipment bag slung over my shoulder. "Fine. Go ahead," the guard said. He didn't even check the bag.

I tried to appear calm on the outside. But on the inside, I was excited. *Wow, Lord,* I thought. *Thank You!*

Our group spent about half an hour with President Fernando de la Rúa. While Ed and the others presented him with a gift of medical supplies and other materials, I walked around the room snapping pictures. The president's photographer even helped me find a better angle for my photos. I shot three rolls of film during our visit; one of my photos of the president wound up on the front page of an Argentine newspaper.

"Chuck, you were meant to be there today," Ed told me later. "We've been planning that visit with the president for months. But we forgot all about a camera."

Every year after that trip, Ed invited Kathi and me to accompany him on his annual visits to Argentina. But we didn't sense the Lord's blessing to return until five years later. Kathi wasn't able to go, but in 2005 my brother-in-law, Richard, and I accepted Ed's offer.

A few days before our departure in October, a group of us prayed in our home about the trip. As we prayed, I felt the Lord impressing a single word on me: *government.* At about the same time, Richard received a vision from God. It was a picture of a government official kneeling and repenting.

We didn't understand the meaning of these messages from the Lord, but we figured He would let us know when the time was right.

On our first full day in Argentina, our fifteen-member group traveled to a government building in one of the provinces. There we joined fifteen government officials, along with a camera crew, and met a leading member of the province's House of Representatives.

Everyone in our group sat down at a long conference table in the lead official's office; the other government representatives stood behind us. I was in the middle; the official sat at the end. Our group leaders presented him with a container of medical supplies, which was followed by a round of document-signing that signified acceptance of our gift. Then he addressed us, thanking us for our generosity. Dave Thompson, one of our group leaders, translated his words into English.

I watched this powerful man closely as he spoke. He was a commanding presence. He wore a suit and tie, was bald on top, and had a thin mustache. He seemed very comfortable being at the center of attention.

Suddenly, an image broke into my thoughts. It was of a government official on his knees, repenting.

Oh, no, Lord, I thought. *This is only our first full day here. We have a whole week ahead of us. Are You sure this is the one?*

Of course He was sure.

Then I sensed another strong impression. It was the thought, *He has to repent.*

Repent for what? I wondered. *And how am I going to get him on his knees?*

The government official completed his speech, and Dave finished his translation. Before our meeting that day, Dave had talked about the spiritual opportunity ahead of us. "I trust you guys," he said. "If one of you gets a word from the Lord, we're going with it."

Now Dave was looking around the table. "Does anyone here have a word from the Lord?" His gaze rested on me.

I didn't want to do it. It would have been easier to close my eyes, sit like a statue, and let the moment pass. But for some reason, words came out of my mouth.

"Yeah, I do," I said.

As Dave translated my words into Spanish, my mind moved on fast forward. *OK, Lord, what are we going to do here now? You'd better give me something.*

An image came to me. It was a moment from a few weeks earlier, back in Elk River. Duane Kropuenske and I and some of the other executives from Riverview Community Bank were sitting around a long table in our boardroom. I was praying.

I turned to address the head official. "I am the vice president of a bank in the United States. The bank's leaders and I recently invited Jesus Christ to sit at the head of our table and be the overseer and CEO of our bank. Would you be willing to invite Jesus Christ to sit at the head of *this* table"—I placed my hand on the table surface—"and be the overseer of your congress and your government?"

His answer, after the translation, was simple: "*Sí.*"

OK, Lord, I thought. *But he has to be on his knees, repenting. How are we going to do this?*

Immediately, another revelation filled my mind.

"Since you said yes, that means to me that you have not yet offered that invitation, which also means to me that you need to repent. Would you be willing to repent before the Lord?"

The leader eyed me intently as I spoke. He nodded his head during Dave's translation and again offered a direct answer: "*Sí.*"

Great, I thought. *But he still has to be on his knees!*

I glanced at the dual rows of people lining the table. *There are more than thirty people and a camera crew in this room, Lord. I don't want to embarrass this government official or myself. I don't want to create a scene or start an international crisis on our first day here. But if this is truly what You want, and if You give me the words, I'll keep going.*

The words came.

"Since you are willing to repent, would you be willing to do so in a spirit of repentance by being on your knees? If you are, I'm willing to kneel with you, repent with you, and lead you in a prayer of repentance as we invite Jesus Christ to sit at this table. Would you be willing to do that?"

For the third time, the answer was, "*Sí.*"

I walked to the head of the table and knelt down. The government official joined me, and then everyone pushed back their chairs and got on their knees. As I prayed, the presence of God filled the room.

When we finished, this powerful leader stood and grabbed me for a long embrace. "*Gracias,*" he said. "*Gracias. Gracias.*"

As a visitor to an unfamiliar land and culture, meeting highly influential government officials, I was intimidated by the circumstances. I wanted to make the right impression. Yet a few years before, the Lord had warned me. *I am going to lead you into nations,* He said. *Remember this: The people around the world are no different than the people in Elk River. Some have more money or different titles. But they are just as human. Don't do anything different than what you are doing right here in Elk River. Just listen to Me.*

In Argentina, despite the circumstances, I listened and heard God's voice. Back home in Minnesota, I am happy to say that I am still listening and hearing today.

If you are like most people, you do not want to look foolish. You prefer to be well liked, approved of, and respected by others. Deep down, you are often afraid of saying or doing something that will bring on rejection or ridicule. And that fear grows stronger when you are with someone you really want to impress.

Yet our Lord desires that we be most concerned with His approval, not that of our fellow man. Jesus said, "What I tell you in the dark, speak in the daylight; what is whispered in your ear, proclaim from the roofs. Do not be afraid of those who kill the body but cannot kill the soul" (Matt. 10:27–28).

The fear of what others think of us is an obstacle to spreading the gospel and doing God's will. So be courageous! Regardless of your reputation in the world, He will stand by you to the end.

Chapter Seventeen

AUTHORITY

Principle #17: Act within the authority
God gives you—no more and no less.

Our 757 jet cruised through blue skies at thirty thousand feet, yet I hardly noticed the amazing view. I was preoccupied. I was on my first trip out of the country to Argentina, but that wasn't the reason for my distraction. I was trying to figure out where the Lord was taking me—not just that day, but for the rest of my life.

My job as a mortgage banker was going fine, but more and more often I was being called away for ministry purposes. That was exciting, but I could barely keep up with my business commitments. If this continued, I soon wouldn't have time for a career at all. *Lord, what are You up to?* I prayed. *Are You going to remove me from work completely to go full-time into ministry?*

I pulled a book I'd been reading out of the pocket of the seat in front of me. It was called *God@Work*. I started reading one of the last chapters about another man from Minnesota named Dennis Doyle. Dennis, it seemed, had struggled with the same issue facing me now. He learned that his calling was to stay in the marketplace. He believed God had told him he could do ministry and succeed in business at the same time.

That was the same message God had given me years before. Now, sitting on the plane and reading about Dennis Doyle, I felt He was reminding me of that message. He was telling me I was still where I was supposed to be.

I was so encouraged by the chapter I just read that I immediately prayed, *Lord, I would really like to meet Dennis someday and become friends with him.*

The day after we landed, I looked for Paul Cox, founder of Aslan's Place and another member of the ministry team that had flown to Argentina. I found him in the large conference room of the Buenos

Aires hotel where we were staying. Though I sensed the Lord had spoken to me, I wanted confirmation. We sat down in a corner of the room, where I explained to Paul what I was struggling with and asked him to pray for me.

"Chuck, have you ever been anointed as a pastor in the marketplace?" he said.

"No, I haven't."

"Then we need to do that."

Paul had a bottle of anointing oil with him. He dabbed a small amount on his finger, traced the image of a cross on my forehead, and prayed for my role before God as a pastor in my business life. It took only a few minutes, but it was as if a light turned on in my mind. *Yeah, that is me,* I thought. *A marketplace pastor. That makes sense.*

As Paul finished, a worship service began at the other end of the room. I walked over to the front of the stage where a group of worship singers and musicians were gathered. Soon, more than a hundred people filled the room.

Suddenly I heard God speaking to me: *I want you to prostrate yourself before Me.*

Right there, I lay down on the floor and closed my eyes. A vision like a movie began playing in my head. I was lying down in darkness. Before me were seven rising steps. I lifted my head to see where the steps led, and there, sitting on a golden throne, was Jesus. Brilliant light shone all around Him. He looked down at me, and with two fingers beckoned me forward.

I rose and stepped toward Him. Now light was all around me. I tried to keep my knees from shaking.

A crown leaned against Jesus' throne. He picked it up and stood. Then He motioned with a flat hand for me to put my head down, and He placed the crown on me.

Chuck, He said, *this crown represents the authority I have given you to go into your sphere of influence in the marketplace. I want you to take this authority, go into the places I have called you to go, and use it to tear down the strongholds that the enemy places before you.*

I glanced around me. On the floor surrounding the throne were hundreds, maybe thousands, of golden crowns. "Lord, thank You for what You just did for me," I said. "But I'm confused. What are all these other crowns doing here?"

Turn around, Jesus said. He put His left hand on my shoulder and pointed into the darkness with His right. In the shadows, I could see the outlines of figures moving away.

My children have walked away from the throne and the authority I want to give them, He said. *Others have received their crowns, brought them back, and left them here. They said, "It's too hard" or "I can't do this." I want you to call them back to the throne to receive their crowns.*

Wow, I thought. *Here is my commission from God.*

There is only one time when you will lay your crown down, Jesus said. *That is when you come to worship Me. Don't forget to take it with you when you leave.*

I glanced at the face of the Lord. I was too nervous to look for long. I saw a distinguished yet soft face, one that I instantly knew cared for me.

You have received your crown, Jesus said. *Now go.*

The vision was over. I was "back" in the conference room. But now I was really excited. The Lord had taken away any doubt about what I was supposed to be doing. I didn't know the specifics, but I understood the path He wanted me to take. And He had given me new authority to follow that path.

Later that week, Megan Doyle, the wife of Dennis Doyle, approached me at the hotel. She was a guest speaker at the conference being held at the Buenos Aires hotel. Someone had told her about the vision I had.

"Chuck, I believe you have a prophetic gift," she said. "My husband has had a very similar vision to yours. I would love for you to meet him someday."

A few months later, I did, and Dennis offered to pray and become an intercessor for me. The Lord answered my prayer on the plane.

About a year after my vision about the crowns, I was home asleep when something awakened me in the middle of the night. I realized it was the Lord. "Lord, what do You want?" I said.

Come into this room, He said.

I climbed out of bed and walked to our family room. There in the darkness, I saw a silhouette of Jesus standing just a few feet away. Immediately, I was uneasy. I love hearing the Lord's voice, but seeing Him in person is an unnerving experience.

He gave me the same command He had given me during the vision in Argentina: *Prostrate yourself before Me.*

I dropped to the floor. As I lay there, I couldn't help thinking, *Lord, what are You doing here?*

Then the Lord said, *Kneel.* I did.

Now give Me the sword I gave you. Years before, in a vision, the Lord had given me a huge sword to carry in a scabbard on my back. It was double-bladed, with a gold handle studded with jewels.

There in my family room, with my left hand, I reached over my back to where I knew the sword would be. I gently handed it to the Lord.

"Lord," I said, "what are You going to do with the sword?"

I'm going to knight you.

"Knight me?" I said, surprised. "Where is that in Scripture?"

It's a prophetic act, He said. *You are my warrior. I am going to bestow a higher level of authority on you. Even the demons will recognize this authority.*

Just like in the King Arthur stories, Jesus placed the blade of the sword on my shoulder and knighted me. *Now stand up,* He said, *and step forward.*

We were already so close that we were almost touching. "But Lord," I said, "if I step forward—"

Yes, He said. *If you step forward, you will be in Me, and I will be in you.*

I stepped into the Lord. As I did, He seemed to dissolve. Then He was gone.

The next morning, I told Kathi what had happened. She was amazed. Then she asked, "Did you see the newsletter from Rick Joyner?"

I hadn't. Rick is the founder of MorningStar Ministries in South Carolina. Kathi brought the newsletter to me, and I read Rick's words: "God is out knighting His warriors." It was confirmation that my vision was from Him.

More recently, after we launched Riverview Community Bank, I thought about the increasing number of ministry opportunities in my life. For some reason, it seemed I was able to touch many more lives than I had years earlier. "Lord," I prayed, "why am I able to do so much more today than before?"

Chuck, because I have all authority, I respect authority. In your previous places of employment, you could not go beyond the authority of whom you were working for. Today, at the bank, you have all authority. You're a founder and stockholder. One of your bank vision statements is to bring Christianity into the marketplace, and the bank has released you to do these things. You can operate in all authority.

I realized what an important truth I had just learned, especially for someone trying to minister to others in the marketplace. Some businesspeople, out of their enthusiasm for God, will overstep their position. They may walk into someone's office and begin praying for another person or that business without permission to do so. That approach may do more harm than good. It may offend the other person and make him less open to the Lord. And because they have no authority to pray, God is less likely to act on their requests.

Others, particularly those in positions of leadership, may give away their spiritual authority. If a manager knows of a conflict between two employees, for instance, he may ignore it or rely only on secular problem-solving techniques to resolve the situation. But if he first takes the matter to the Lord in prayer, he has more power at his disposal than he can imagine.

Today, when I am speaking to an audience, the Lord often instructs me to tell the story of my vision about the crowns. He wants me to talk about the importance He places on authority. I ask the crowd to stand, close their eyes, put their hands out, and invite Jesus to come to them with the crown He has made for each one. Then I end with a prayer: "Lord, as we stand before You, would You do for each person here what You did for me? I call for greater authority to be on their heads as it was for me."

Then I address the audience: "Now, I take the authority that God has given me and I release you to go into your destiny. I release a spirit of obedience upon you, and I release you into the places that God has called you to go. Now walk with authority. Amen."

Jesus leaves no doubt about who has ultimate authority under any circumstances: "All authority in heaven and on earth has been given to me" (Matt. 28:18). But the Bible also makes it clear that as long as we are not asked to violate God's law, we are also to respect the authority of our fellow men. We are told, "Obey your leaders and submit to their authority" (Heb. 13:17). And the apostle Paul writes, "Everyone must submit himself to the governing authorities, for there is no authority except that which God has established" (Rom. 13:1).

God's ways bring peace to our hearts and order to our lives, and one of the keys to understanding His will is to recognize the significance of authority. We must be careful not to overstep the authority given to us. But when the Lord grants us authority and gives us direction on what to do, we please Him by using that authority and bringing glory to Him.

Chapter Eighteen

I Knew You Would Call

Principle #18: When the world calls,
simply tell them the truth.

I walked into my corner office just before 8:00 a.m. and took a deep breath. In front of me was a desk, an executive chair behind it, a bookcase, and a laptop computer. Everything was new. It was March 3, 2003, or "030303" for those who like working with numbers. It was also opening day for the mortgage loan operation of our new business, Riverview Community Bank. I wanted to get started on the right foot, so I closed the door and sat down to pray.

"OK, Lord, here we are," I said. "What's going to happen? How are You going to use me and this bank to bring glory to You?"

It wasn't long before I had an answer: *Chuck,* the Lord said, *I'm going to cause such an acceleration of growth in your life that the secular world is going to take notice. You're going to be invited to speak. When the world calls, simply tell them the truth.*

"I agree with these words, Lord, and I receive them," I said. I didn't know exactly what His message meant, but I knew I would find out.

And over the next year, I did find out. I saw just how much the Lord intended to bless our new venture. The bank's deposits and assets increased at an incredible rate, and so did our reputation as "the bank that prays for people."

That is why I wasn't too surprised by the phone call I received during the summer of 2004. The *New York Times Magazine* was doing a story about the faith-at-work movement, and my friend Os Hillman, founder and head of Marketplace Leaders and the International Coalition of Workplace Ministries, recommended that they talk to me.

I was wary at first. Why would the *New York Times Magazine* want to do a positive story about God? But I became more comfortable with the idea.

Over a day and a half that August, the bank staff, members of the community, and I were interviewed. The photographers and reporters were with me when I prayed for a couple whose ministry was on the verge of bankruptcy. They joined me for a Pray! Elk River meeting at the library. They had dinner with Kathi and me at our home.

I didn't try to impress them or do anything different than usual. I explained that we considered Riverview a Christian financial institution, that we invited Jesus to be our CEO, and that we prayed with customers. I said that I sometimes slipped and told people, "Come on over to the church—I mean, the bank." I described our prayer activity in the Elk River community.

The article was originally scheduled to appear in the *New York Times Magazine* in mid-November 2004. But in October, I learned that the schedule had changed. There was a scramble to move it up, and "Faith at Work" became the cover story for the October 31 issue, reaching five million readers.

The next day, I received a call from a television producer in France. A few days before, he had been assigned to do a show about faith in America. Then he saw the *New York Times Magazine* article. He wanted to interview me for his show. I agreed.

Two days after the *New York Times Magazine* article came out, George W. Bush was reelected president of the United States by a narrow margin. Many credited his ability to connect with Christian voters for his victory, which brought new attention to the issue of faith in America and the faith-at-work movement.

Now the world was calling almost daily. I received interview requests from the *London Times* newspaper, Germany's two largest newspapers, a German television network, one of Japan's largest newspapers, the Canadian Broadcast Corporation, and the *National*

Post newspaper in Canada. In America, I heard from CBS, CNBC, PAX television, National Public Radio, *Good Housekeeping* magazine, and newspapers from across the country. In each case, I tried to simply tell the "God stories" as they happened.

The producer from France interviewed me personally in Elk River. His show on faith in the workplace, part of a three-part series about faith in America, aired in France and other parts of Europe in November 2005. While the show was being broadcast there, I received a phone call from a businessman inviting me to come to Paris to speak at his church. "I'm watching you on TV as I'm speaking to you!" he said.

Another man who flew out to interview me in person was a Japanese reporter. He represented a Tokyo newspaper that reached eight million readers daily.

After we finished the interview in my office, I sensed the Lord telling me to probe further into his heart. I said, "We've just talked about how I pray with my customers and many other people I meet. Can I pray for you, too?"

"Well, I'm Buddhist," he said.

"That may be true," I said. "But I can still pray for you, can't I?"

The Japanese reporter thought that over. "All right," he said.

When I was finished praying, he said, "Mr. Ripka, thank you so much. You are the first Christian that has ever prayed for me."

That night, he sent me an e-mail saying that he had been a little depressed during our interview because he had lost the watch his wife had given him as a wedding present. He went on to write that when he got back to his hotel room, he found it under his bed. He took it as a sign that God had given him favor because of my prayer. Then he asked if I would be willing to meet with him again. I agreed.

The next night we met at a restaurant near the bank. We had a long dinner together. Our waitress was a young woman I had led to the Lord three months earlier. She asked if I would pray for her again, so I did.

After I finished praying, the reporter and I talked about how I often hear the Lord speaking to me. Then I asked him, "Would you like to hear the voice of God the way I do?"

"I can't," he said. "I'm Buddhist."

"Yes, you can. If you invite Jesus Christ to be Lord of your life, as I have, you can hear Him speak to you as He speaks to me. Would you like that?"

"Yes, I would." And this Buddhist reporter closed his eyes and prayed for Jesus to come into his life.

All of this was quite a change for a small-town Minnesota guy like me. Suddenly I was in the limelight, but I knew the attention had nothing to do with me. God had told me that the secular world would take notice. Now the Lord was using me, just as He said He would, to take His name to the nations.

I didn't mind talking to the reporters. I enjoyed telling them about what God was doing. But my favorite calls were from people letting me know how my God stories had encouraged them.

One of those calls came while I was at home, a few months after the *New York Times Magazine* article came out. It was a woman from Singapore.

"The Lord said to me a while back that I was supposed to build a restaurant, and that He was going to use it," the woman said. "But my friends have been telling me, 'You can't do that. God would never bless a restaurant.'

"Then someone told me about you. I looked you up on the Internet, read the *New York Times Magazine* story, and started crying. I realized that if God can use a bank, He can use a restaurant. I just wanted to tell you that and ask if you would pray for me."

God's Word is spreading around the world even as the acceleration in my own life continues. Recently, the Lord told me to start two new global ventures—a ministry we're calling Rivercenter International Network of Christians and a banking enterprise named Rivers International.

When God told me about His latest plan for my life, I was—as usual—uncomfortable. "Lord," I said, "these things are so huge. One by itself would be more than enough. How will I be able to do these things?"

Then He reminded me about His promise to me from years before, that I would be able to do ministry and business at the same time.

That's how you're going to do it with these two ministries in the future, He said.

I realized—once again—that I could trust God. "OK, Lord," I said. "That makes sense."

I don't know what's ahead for my family and me in these new adventures. I know they are going to stretch my faith. But I also know that as long as I am obedient to my Father in heaven, everything else will fall into place.

And to me, that makes a lot of sense.

It's funny how differently we sometimes treat people. When we are with family and friends, we tend to be more casual, more "ourselves." But when we are meeting someone new and "important"—a head of state, a company president, or anyone who is on the "in" list socially—we often change. Suddenly we're more polite. We strive to say intelligent and witty things. We try to elevate ourselves in that person's eyes. And we try to avoid subjects we think they may disapprove of—including God.

The Lord, of course, doesn't want to see us playing these games. He knows what's in every person's heart and isn't impressed by credentials and appearances. He desires to see us be and act as the people He created us to be. And He wants us to speak truth—especially truth about Him.

As the Lord has opened up new opportunities for me to interact with the national and international media and with business and government leaders around the world, I have tried to talk to them in the same way I talk to anyone else in Elk River. Mostly, I tell them about God and what He's doing in my life. And I try to use the same words He uses to communicate with me. That, after all, is truth that everyone needs to hear.

Epilogue

NO LIMITS

Principle #19: Don't try to keep God in a box. He has no limits.

Recently I was having dinner in our home with a friend. He suddenly looked at me with a strange expression. "Chuck, there's an angel standing behind you," he said. "Why don't you listen and see if God has a word for you?"

I hadn't been aware of anything unusual or supernatural happening, but I put my fork down and closed my eyes. Immediately, a vivid picture filled my mind. I was with Kathi, partway up a high cliff next to a waterfall. I saw the Lord standing on top of the cliff. He called Kathi and me up. When we got there, the roar of the waterfall was deafening. I craned my neck to peer over the edge. All I could see was black emptiness.

Then the Lord gave us a one-word command: "Jump."

I took Kathi's hand, and we leaped into the void. It was frightening. We were out of control, a tumbling jumble of arms and feet. I expected to hit the bottom, but we kept falling.

And falling.

And falling.

Finally, however, I began to relax. I got more used to the fall. We were able to stay in one position, feet pointed down. I could hold Kathi's hand again.

"Lord," I said in the vision, "what's going on?"

This is where I want you to be, He said. I know that you trust Me, but when you get comfortable even as you're falling, then I know you really trust Me.

The Lord reminded me of another vision from years earlier. I was in a river with Kathi. The Lord called us out of the river to a high place. Chuck, He said, the reason I have to take you higher is so when you jump into the river, you'll go deeper. I want to take you to a deeper level of trust with Me.

That's exactly what God has been doing with me for years, and continues to do today. He takes me to high places so that He can use me in new ways. I'm never comfortable there. In fact, I'm often petrified. But when I submit to His will, trust that He'll take care of me, and jump, I find that everything is all right. Even as I'm falling, I learn that I can still be comfortable in Him. And the reward of growing closer to God and seeing lives changed for His glory is more fulfilling than I can describe.

Two of the high places the Lord is calling me to next are international banking and ministry enterprises. Their potential—just like God's—is unlimited. I believe God is going to use these new ventures to draw people to Him and change the world in ways I haven't even imagined.

Early in my walk with the Lord, I unconsciously placed limits in my mind on what He was capable of. I put God in a box.

But God is bigger and greater than anything we can comprehend. He doesn't fit in our preconceived models. Only when we put our full trust in His authority and power are we open to His unending possibilities. This is one of the most important lessons the Lord has taught me.

As I look at my life and what I've learned, I can hardly believe the many ways the Lord has blessed me. I've come to realize how much He loves me, and because of His great love, I desire to love and obey Him in return. Yet I know He doesn't want me to keep His love and blessings to myself. He once said to me, Give away what I've given you, because I'm going to give you more.

He wants to give more to you, too.

If you would like to encounter God's great love and discover His unlimited blessings, I invite you to daily obey Him, seek His will, and put your trust in Him. Then watch what happens next.

To get you started, here is a prayer that can change your life:

Father, I ask for forgiveness for turning away from You. I repent for not obeying Your voice and doing things my way. I submit my spirit, soul (mind, will, and emotions), and body to Your will. I love You, Lord. Please help me to grasp how wide and long and high and deep is Your love for me. I ask for Your guidance and wisdom by the Holy Spirit to lead me in all that I am to do. Now I receive all that You have for me in the name of Jesus. Amen.

I believe that you are destined for an eternity of blessings, beginning right now. I know that your next God story is just around the corner.

NOTES

Chapter Nine
No Door Will Be Locked

1. Doug Casey, "Body-Slamming Religion," World Net Daily, July 19, 2001, http://www.worldnetdaily.com/news/article.asp?ARTICLE_ID=23689 (accessed August 24, 2006).